ITALIAN SONGS *for* CLASSICAL GUITAR

2 Carnival of Venice

16 Cicerenella

6 Ciribiribin

12 Come Back to Sorrento

19 Dance of the Hours

26 Funiculi, Funicula

31 I Maccheroni

34 Ideale

39 Italian National Anthem (Fratelli d'Italia)

44 Italian Street Song

56 La Donna È Mobile

53 La Paloma Blanca (The White Dove)

60 Libiamo (Brindisi)

66 Mattinata

69 Musetta's Waltz (Quando Men Vo)

74 O Mio Babbino Caro

86 'O Sole Mio

81 Oh Marie

90 Santa Lucia

96 Serenata

92 Tarantella

99 Vieni Sul Mar

Arrangements by John Hill

ISBN 978-1-61780-370-3

HAL•LEONARD®
CORPORATION

7777 W. BLUEMOUND RD. P.O. BOX 13819 MILWAUKEE, WI 53213

In Australia Contact:
Hal Leonard Australia Pty. Ltd.
4 Lentara Court
Cheltenham, Victoria, 3192 Australia
Email: ausadmin@halleonard.com.au

Visit Hal Leonard Online at
www.halleonard.com

Carnival of Venice

Words and Music by Julius Benedict

Tuning:
(low to high) D-A-D-G-B-E

Moderato con moto

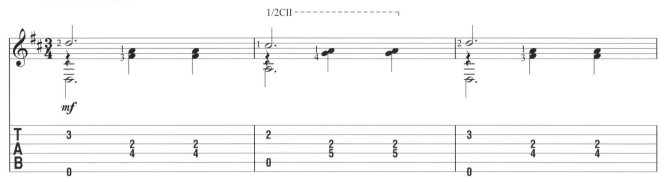

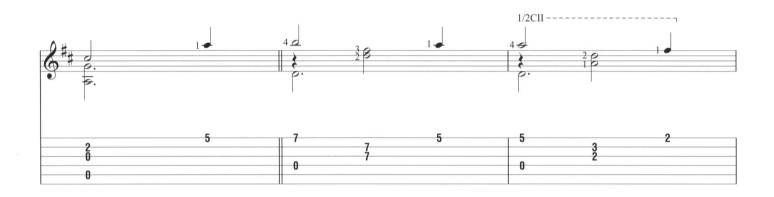

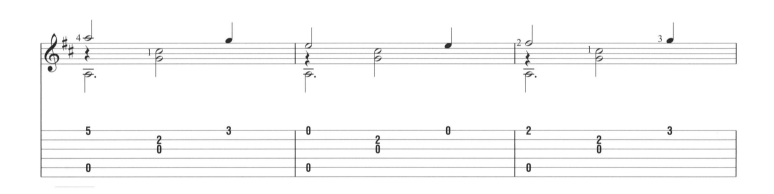

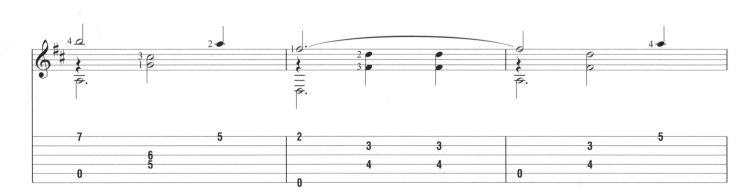

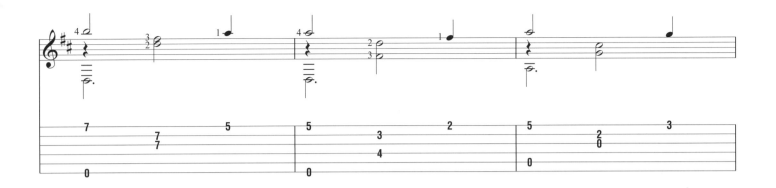

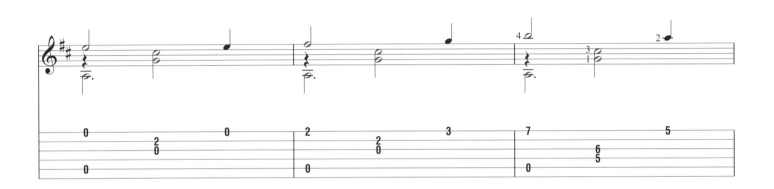

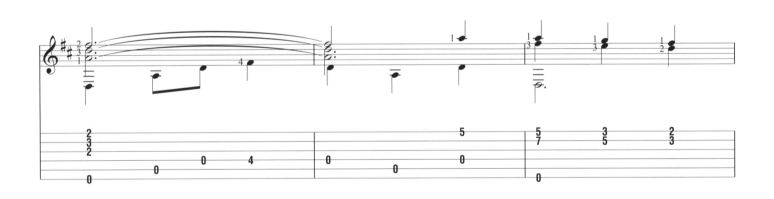

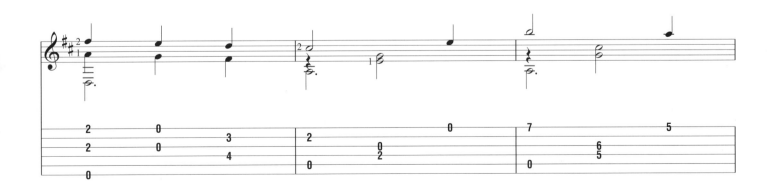

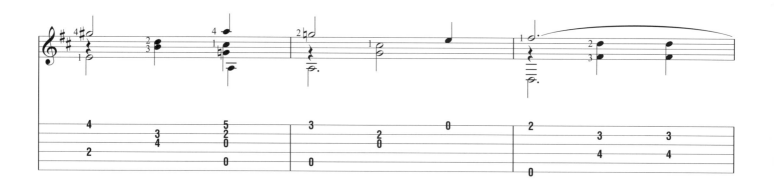

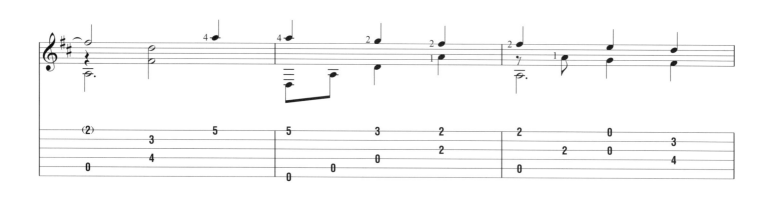

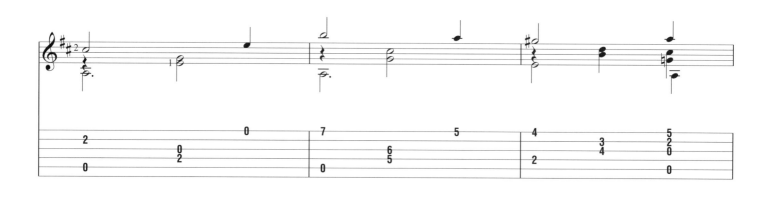

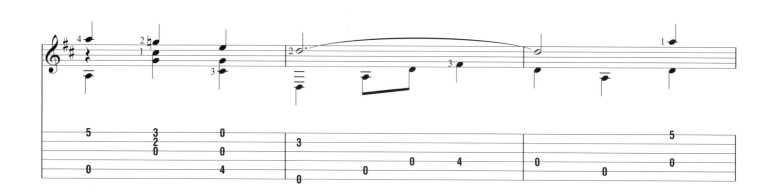

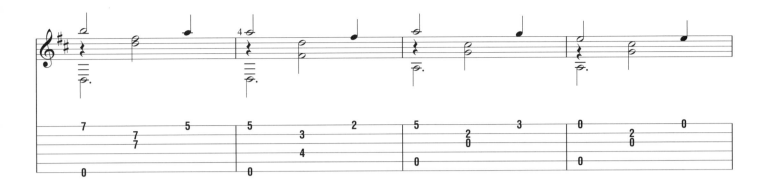

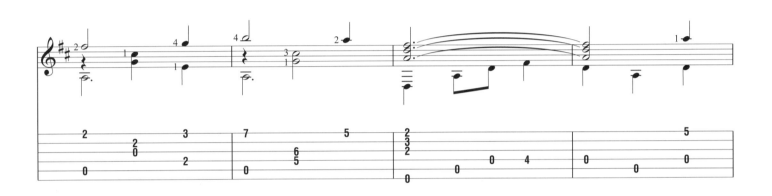

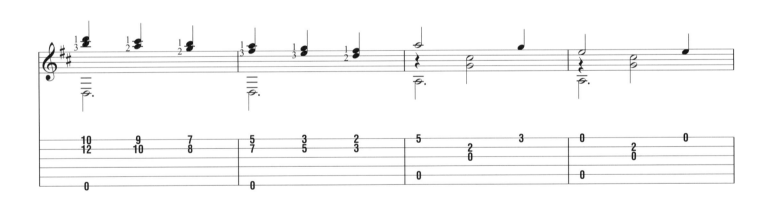

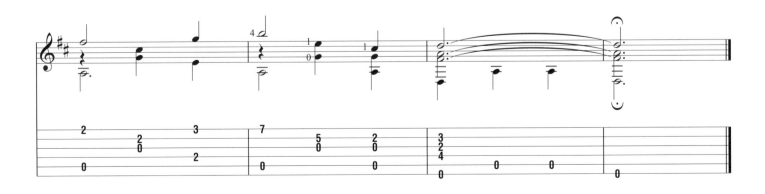

Ciribiribin

Words and Music by Antonio Pestalozza

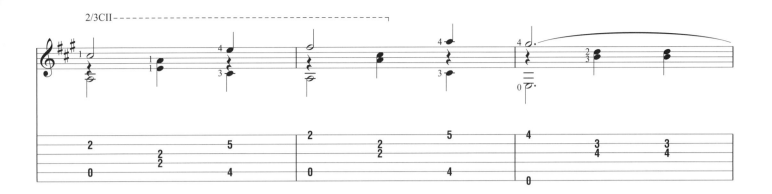

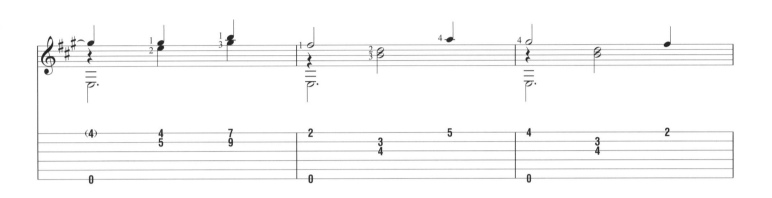

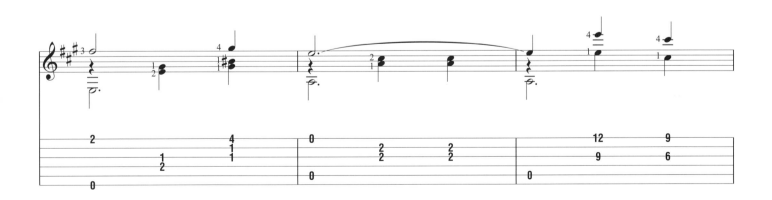

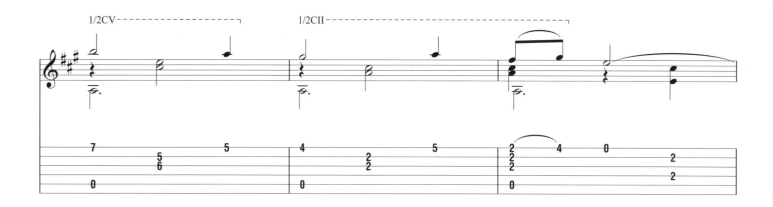

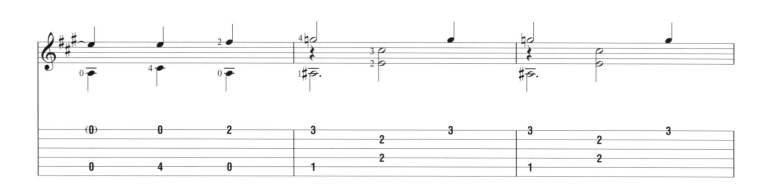

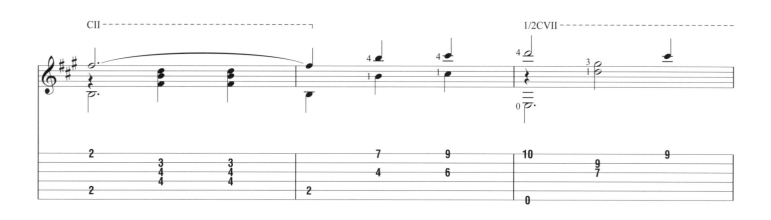

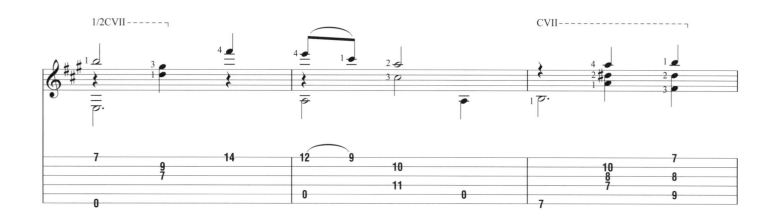

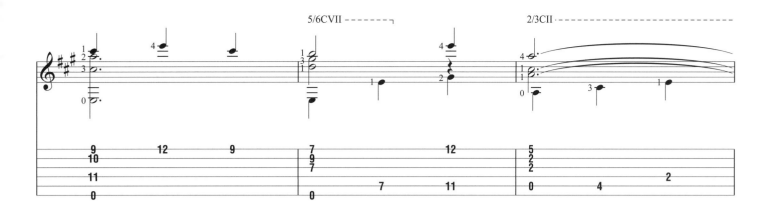

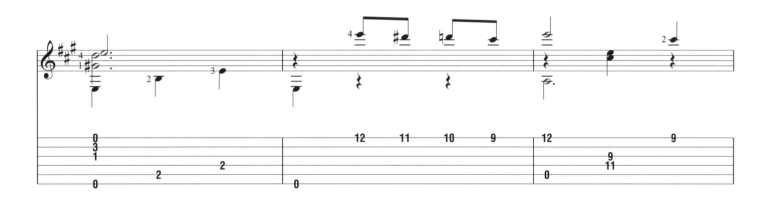

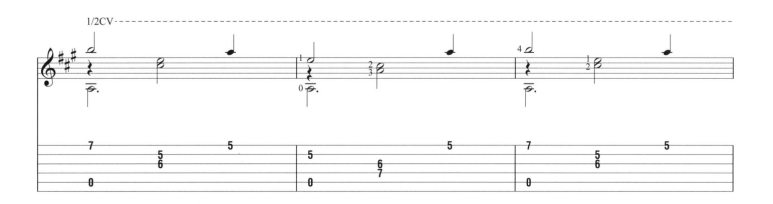

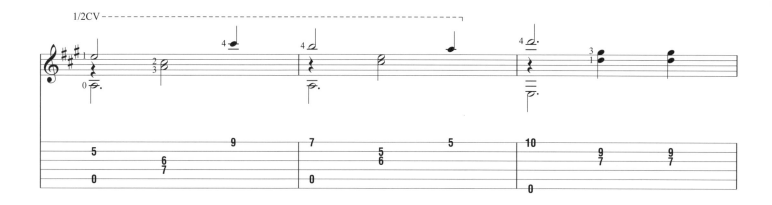

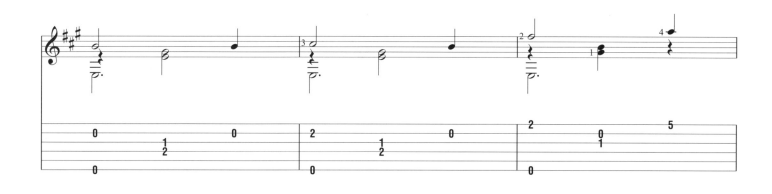

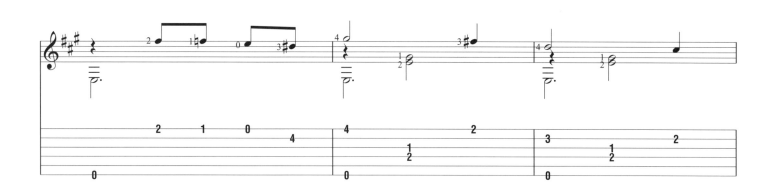

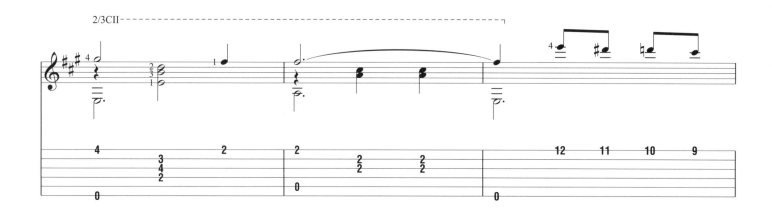

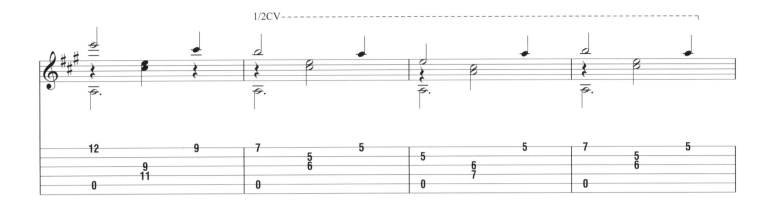

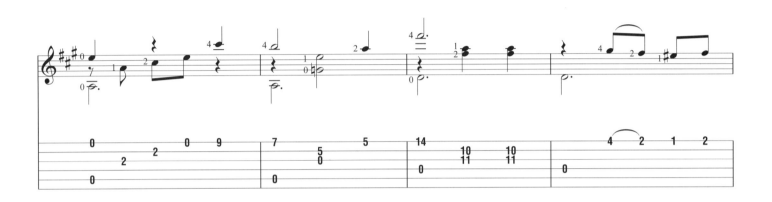

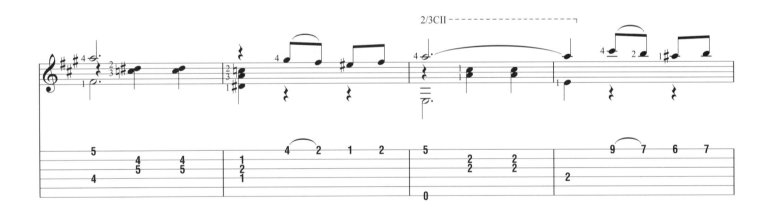

Come Back to Sorrento

By Ernesto de Curtis

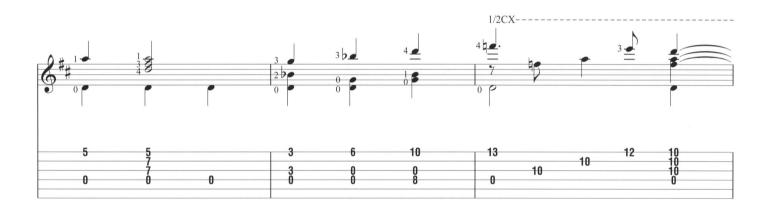

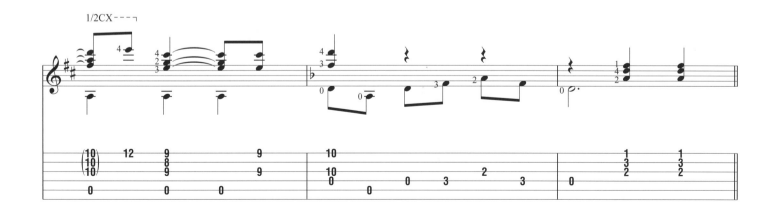

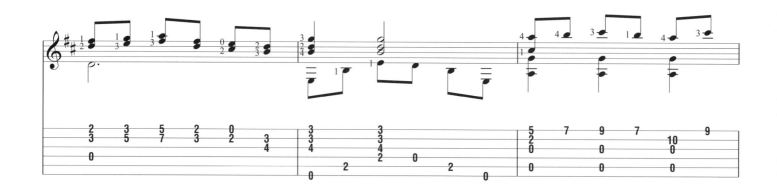

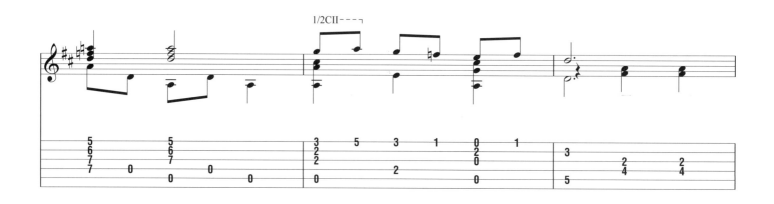

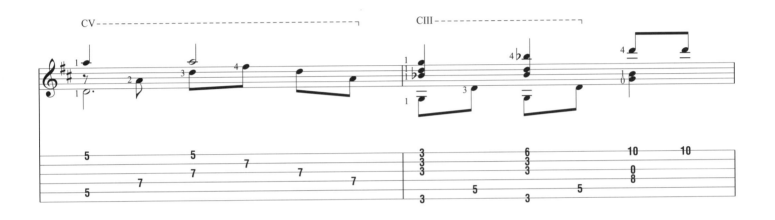

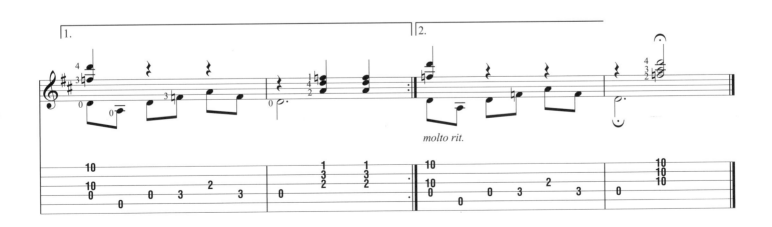

Cicerenella

Neapolitan Song

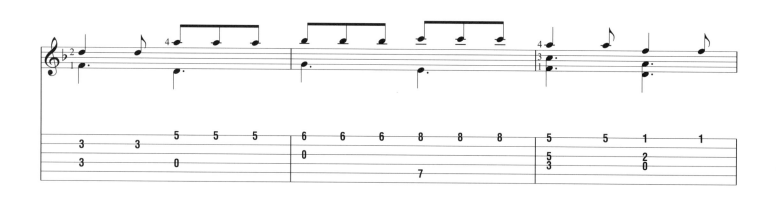

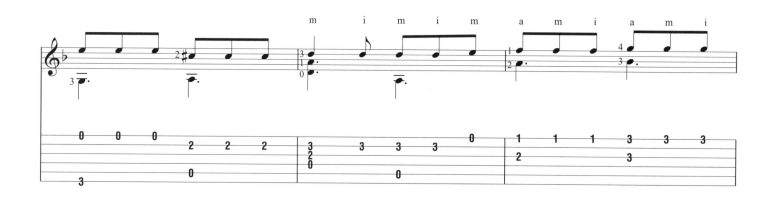

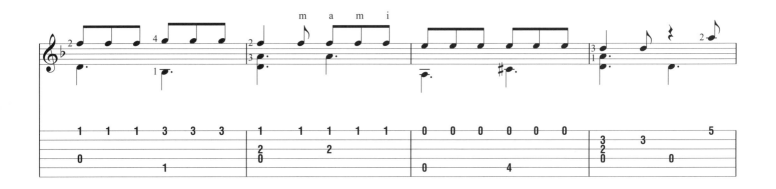

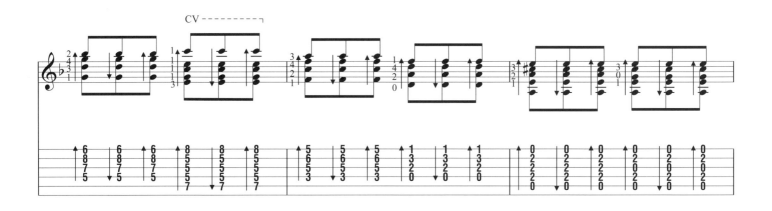

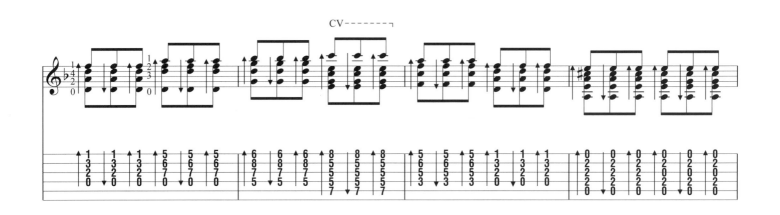

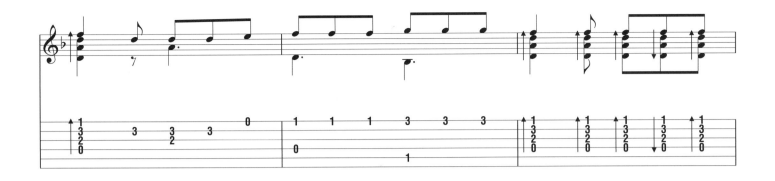

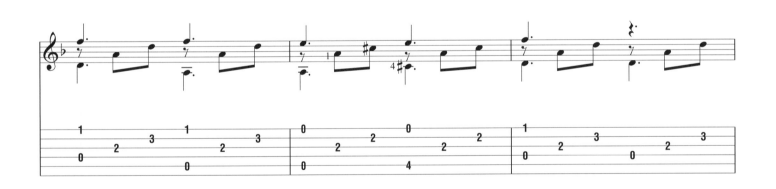

Dance of the Hours

from LA GIOCONDA
By A. Ponchielli

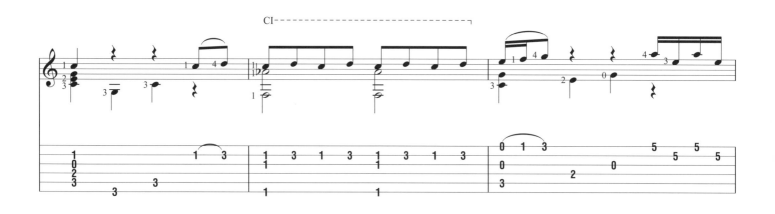

A tempo

poco rit.

A tempo

poco rit.

Entrance of the Hours of the Day

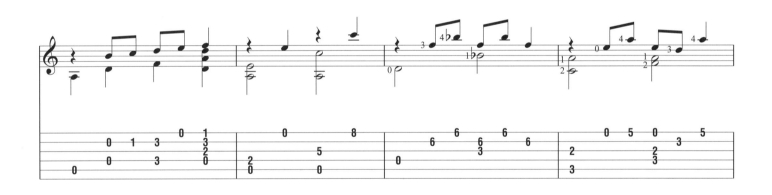

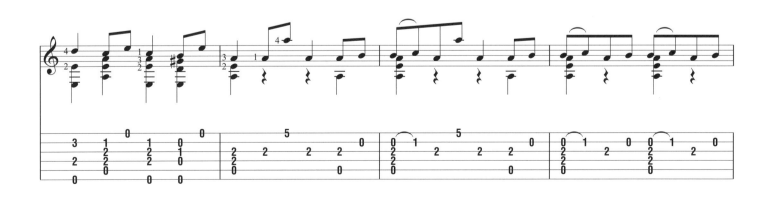

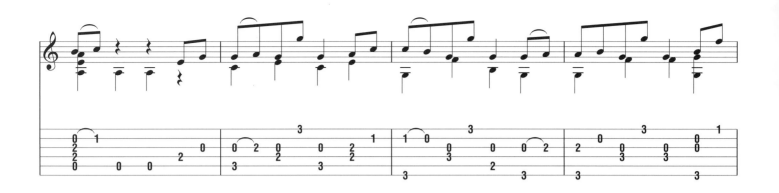

Entrance of the Hours of the Night

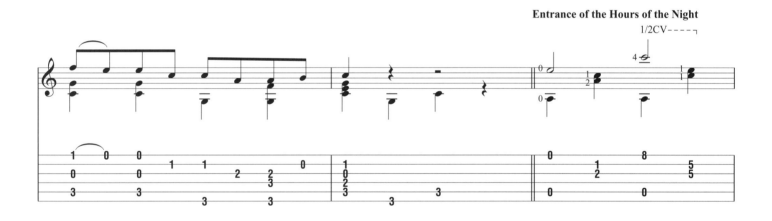

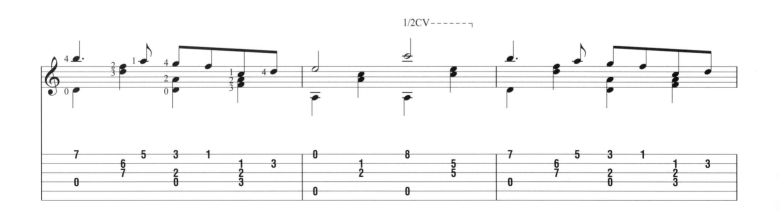

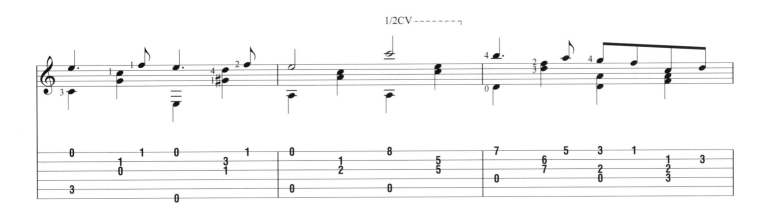

Funiculi, Funicula

Words and Music by Luigi Denza

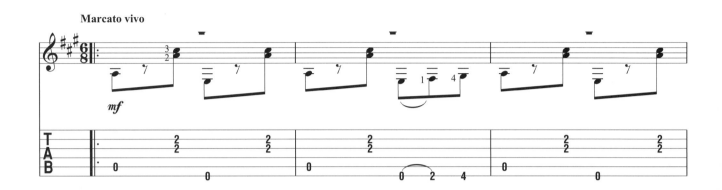

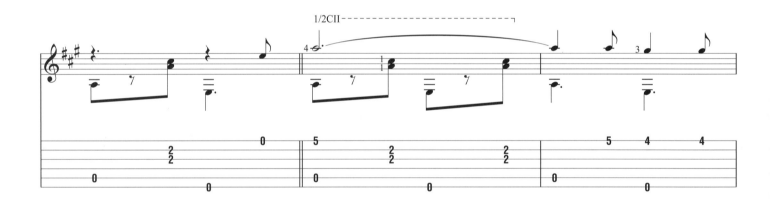

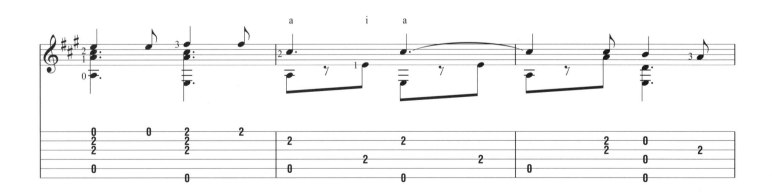

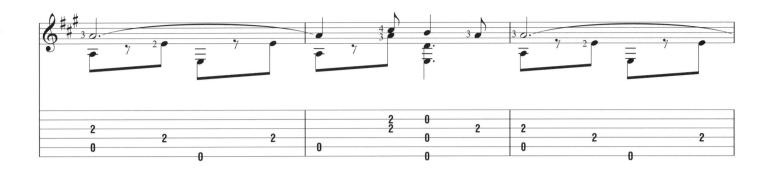

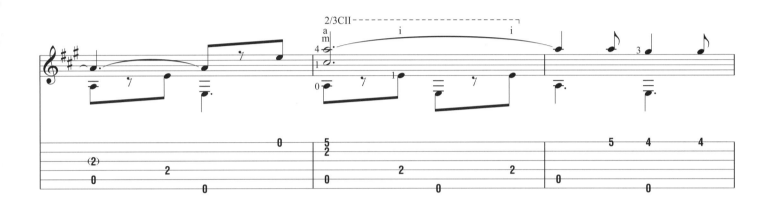

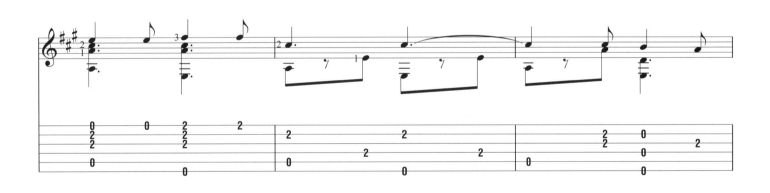

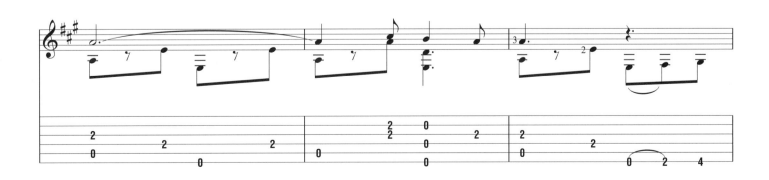

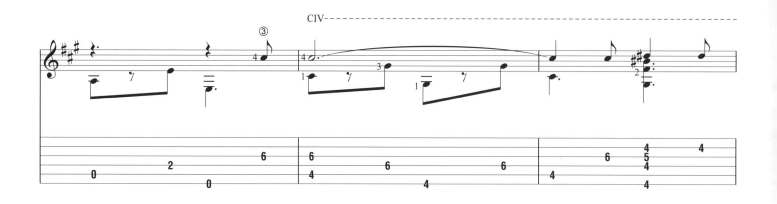

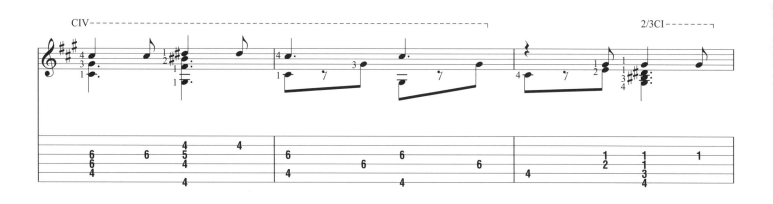

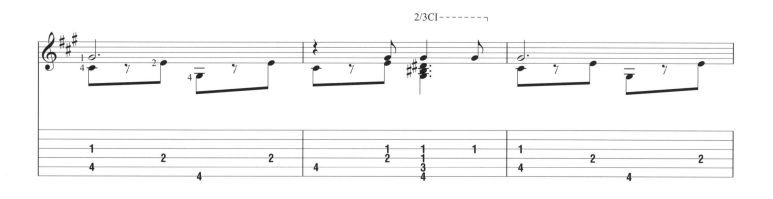

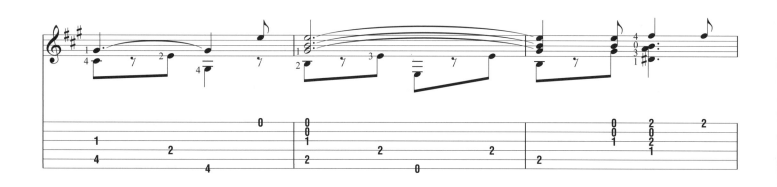

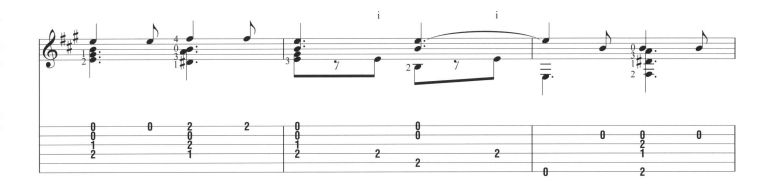

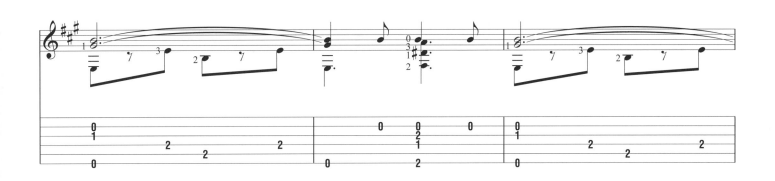

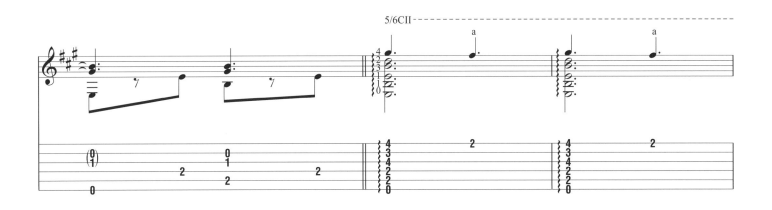

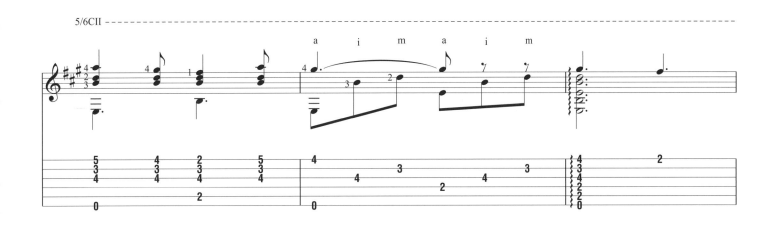

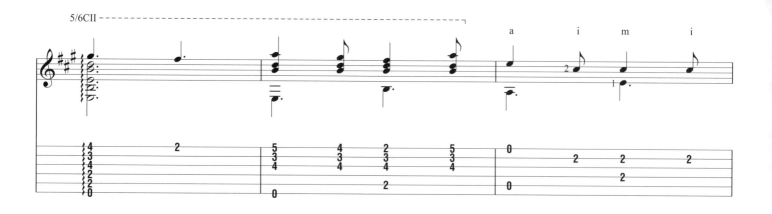

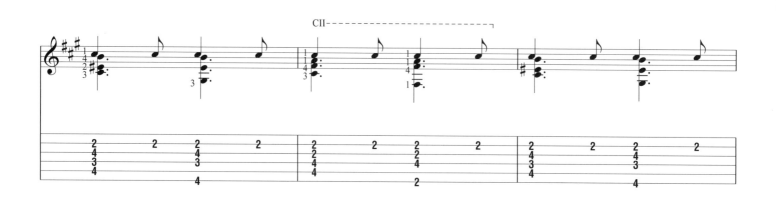

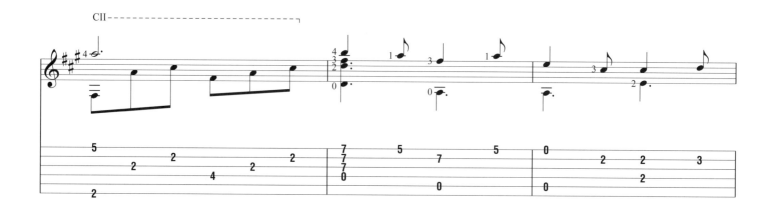

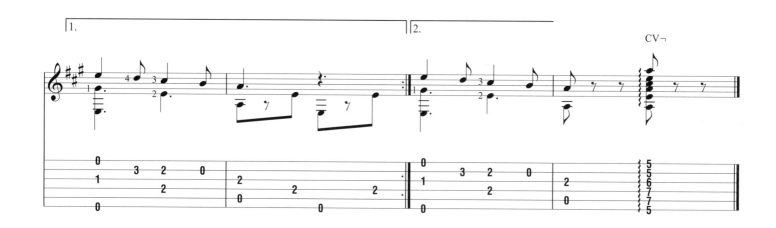

I Maccheroni

Neapolitan Song

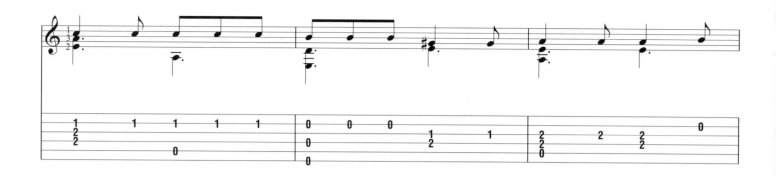

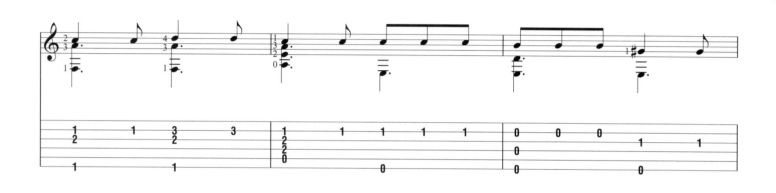

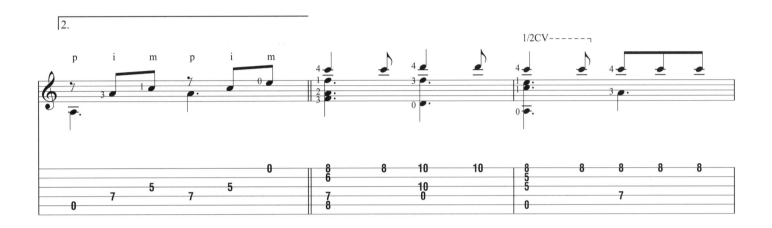

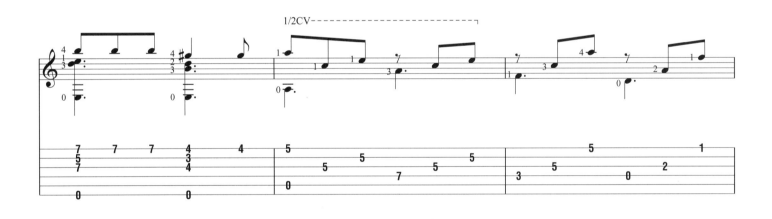

Ideale

Words and Music by Francesco Paolo Tosti

Tuning:
(low to high) D-A-D-G-B-E

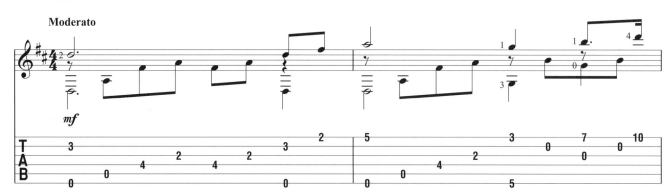

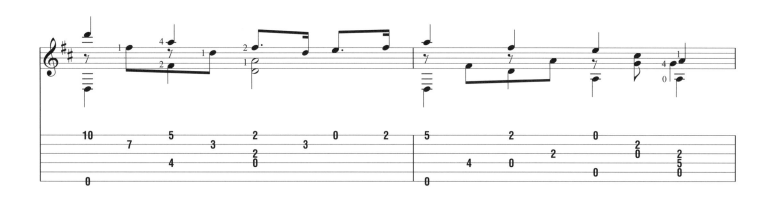

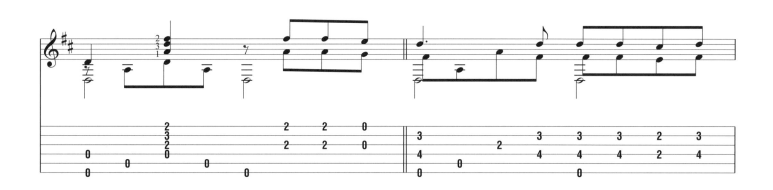

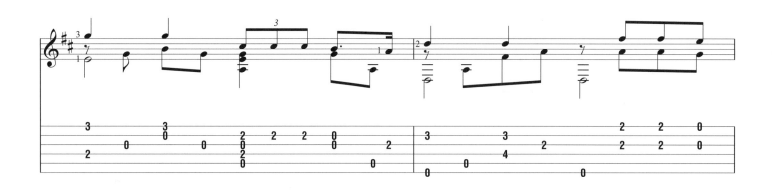

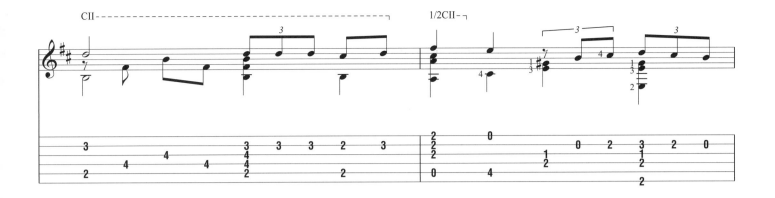

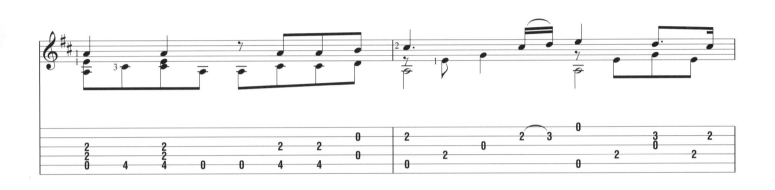

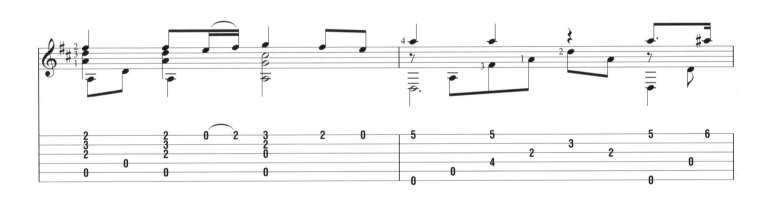

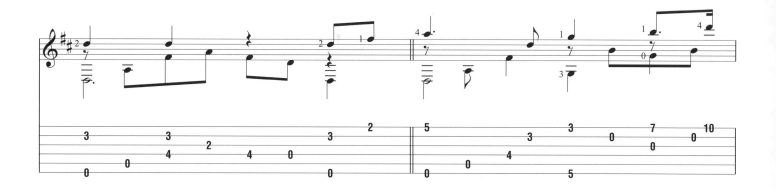

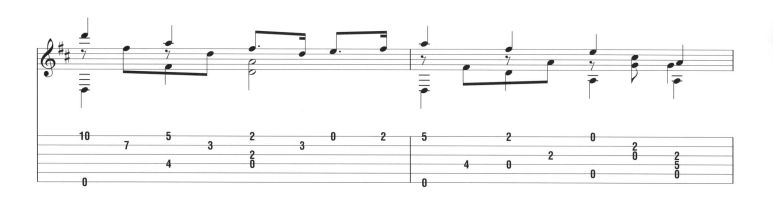

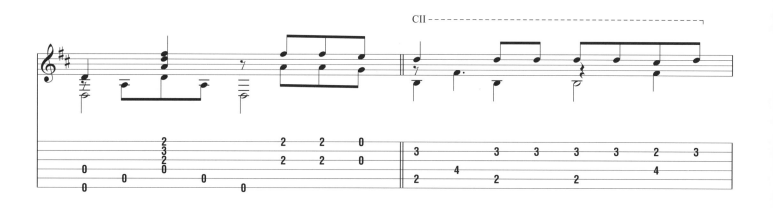

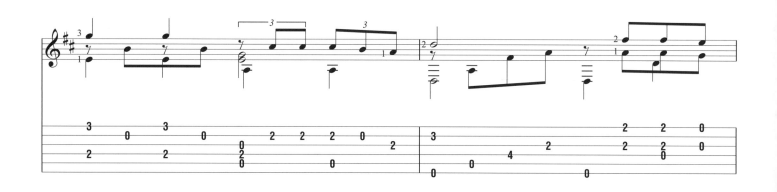

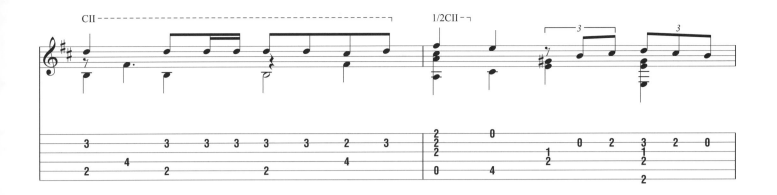

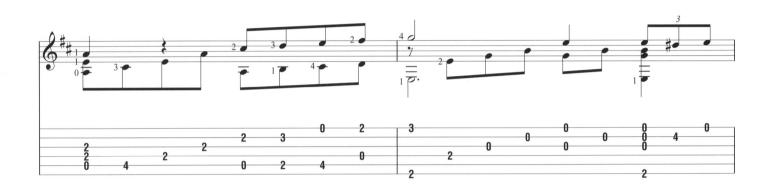

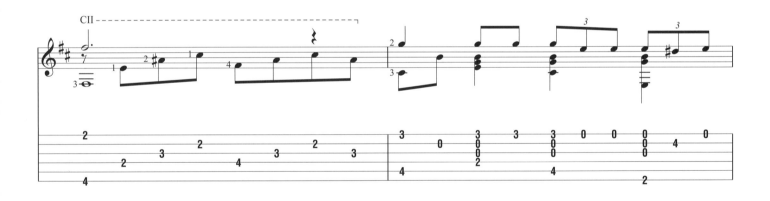

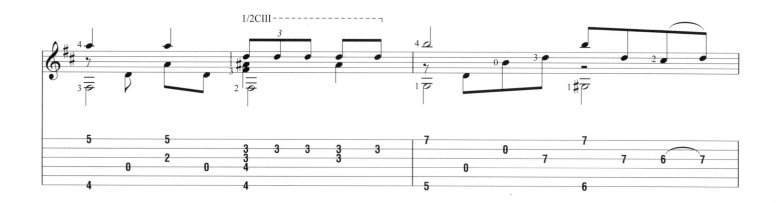

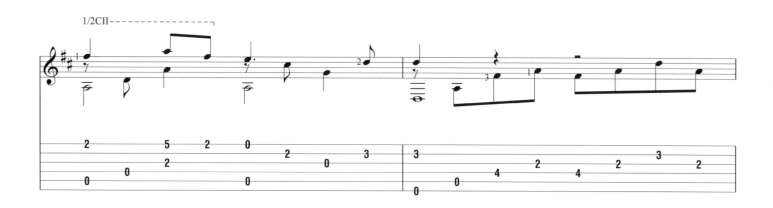

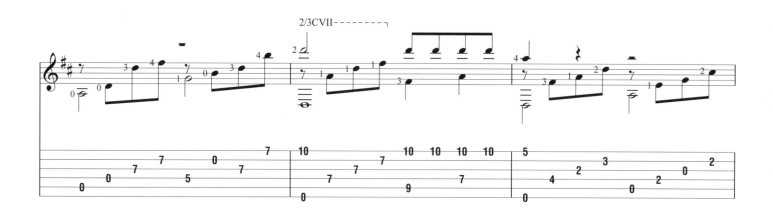

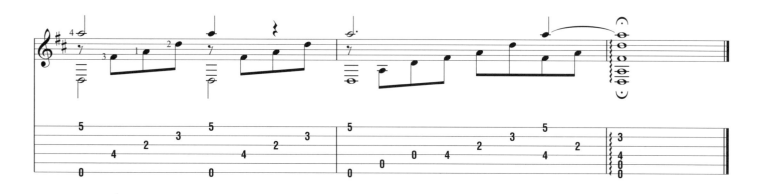

Italian National Anthem
(Fratelli d'Italia)

Words by Goffredo Mameli
Music by Michele Novaro

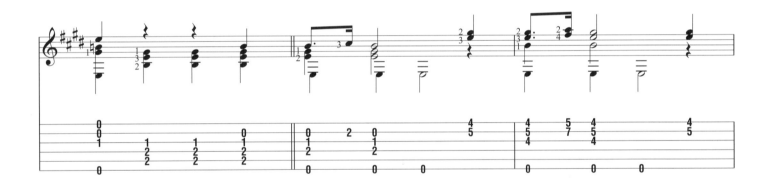

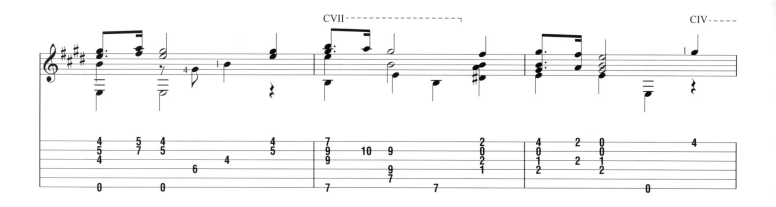

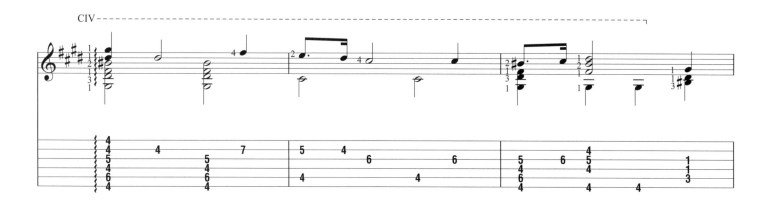

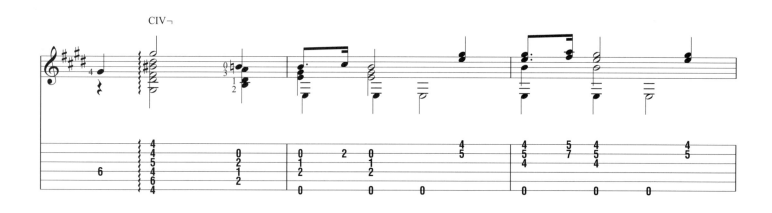

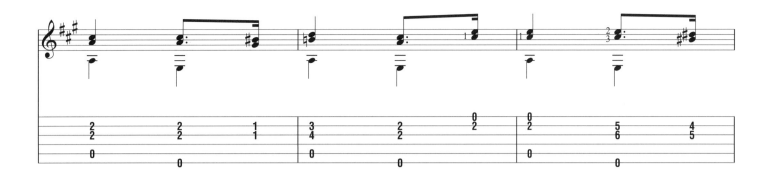

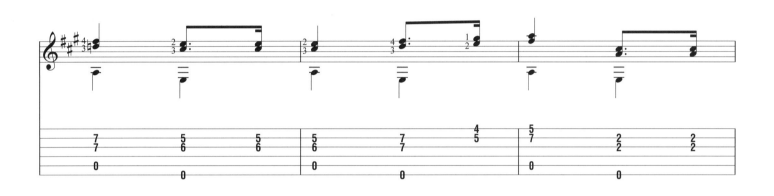

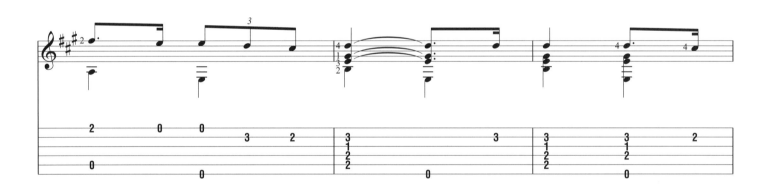

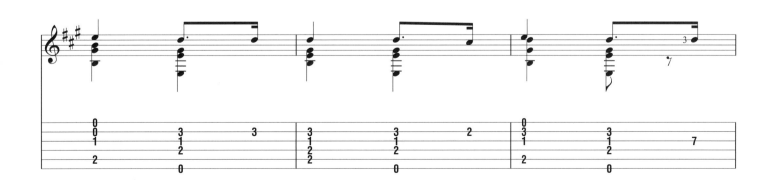

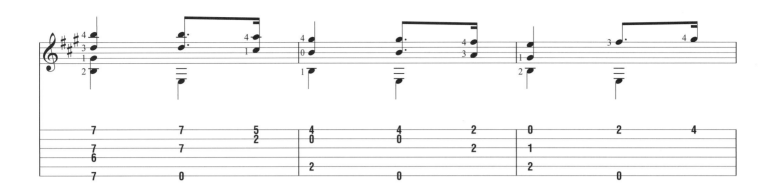

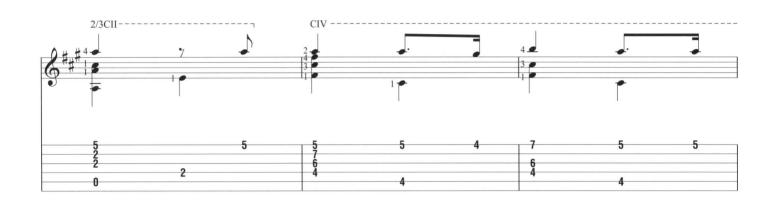

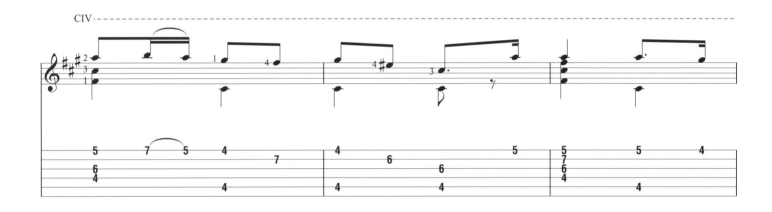

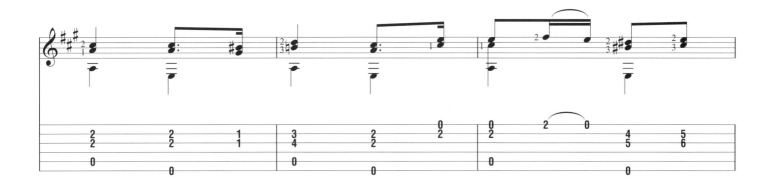

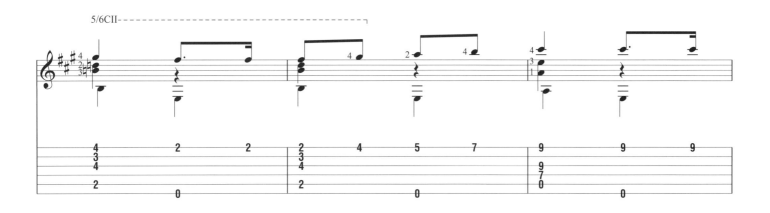

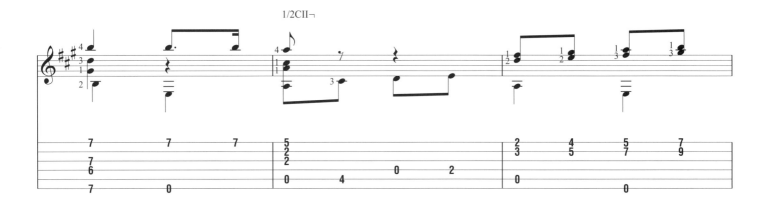

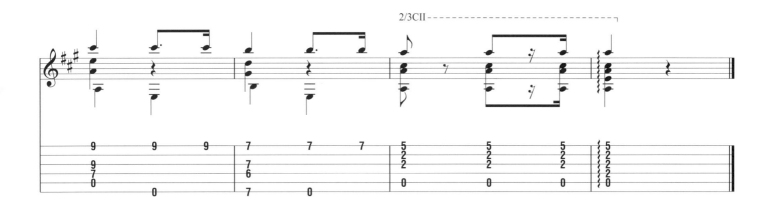

Italian Street Song

from NAUGHTY MARIETTA
Lyrics by Rida Johnson Young
Music by Victor Herbert

Tuning:
(low to high) D-A-D-G-B-E

Moderato

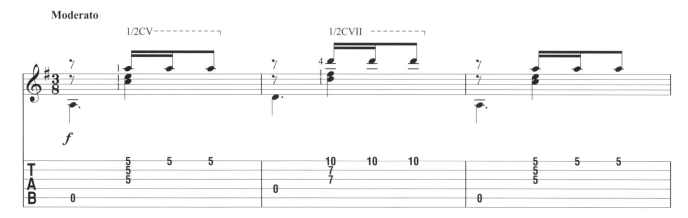

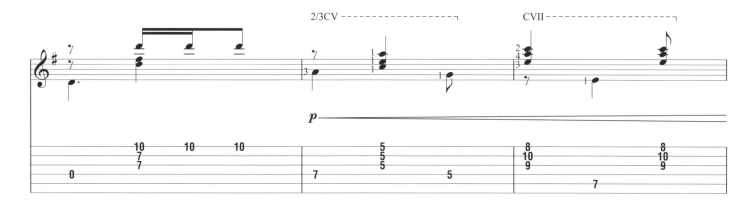

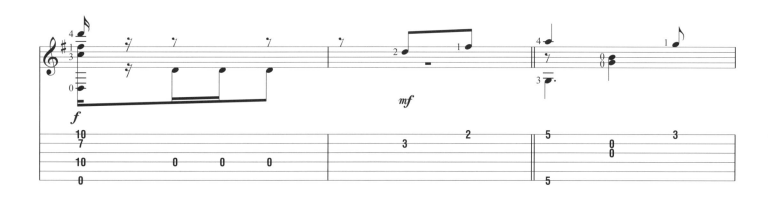

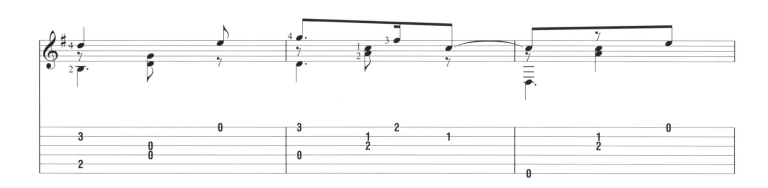

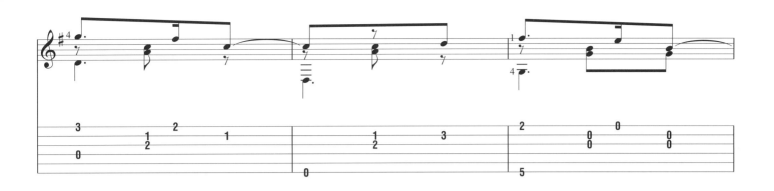

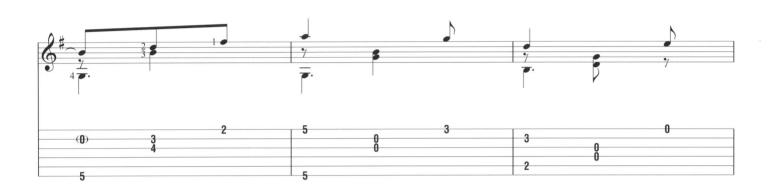

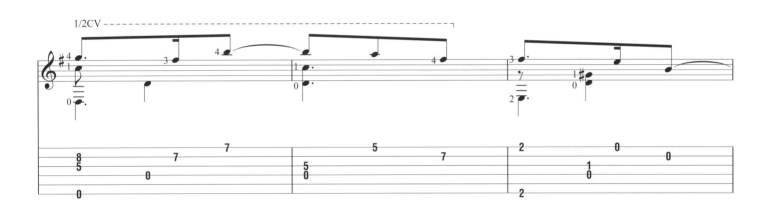

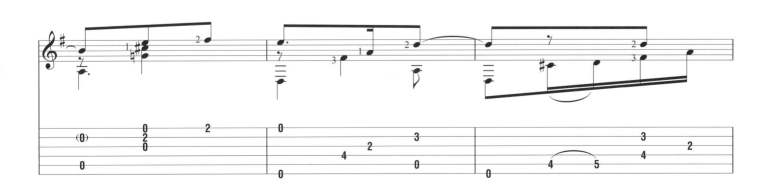

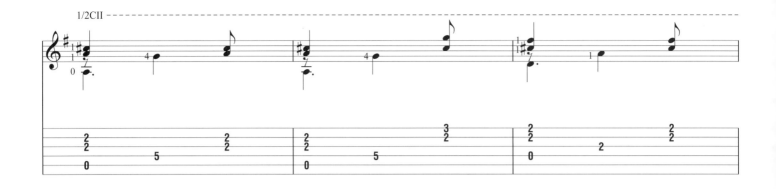

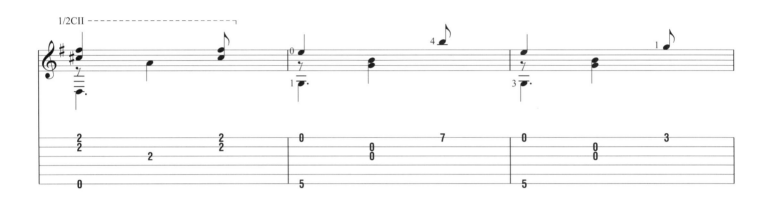

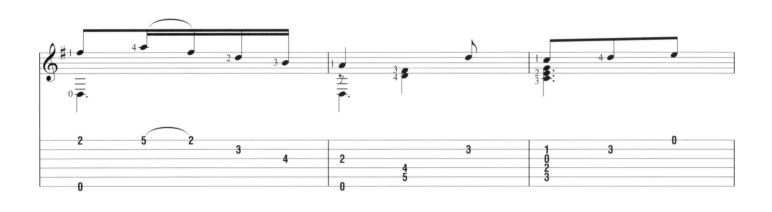

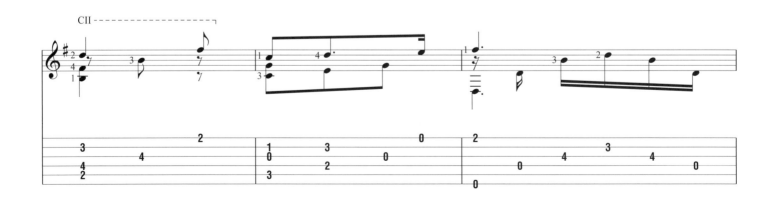

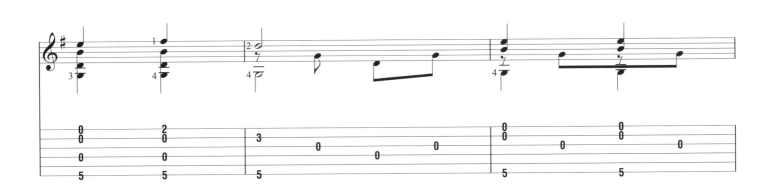

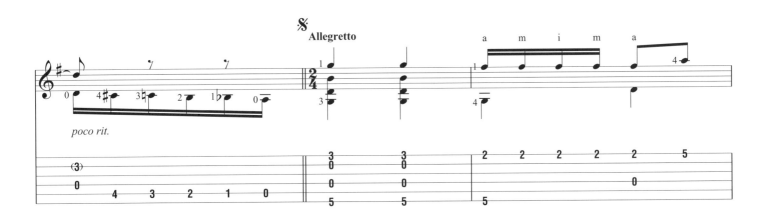

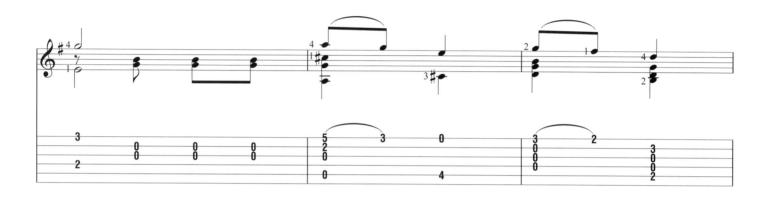

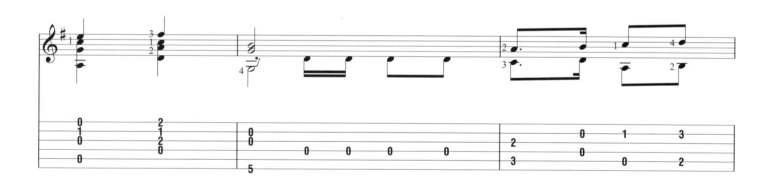

To Coda ⊕

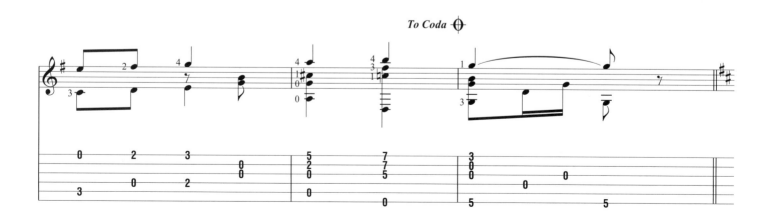

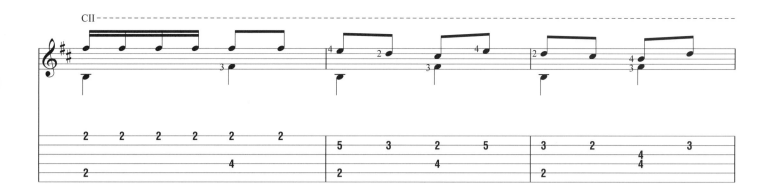

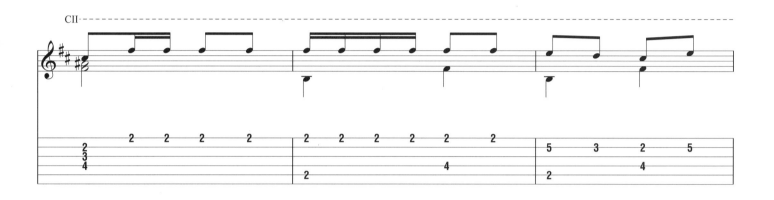

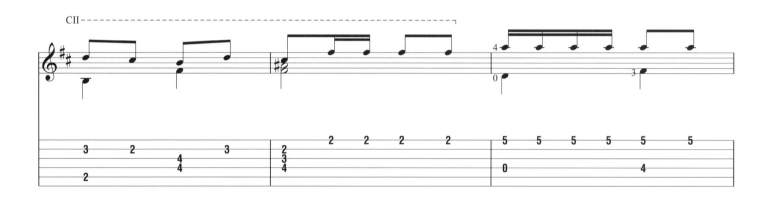

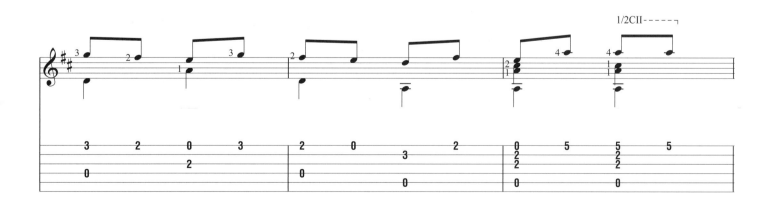

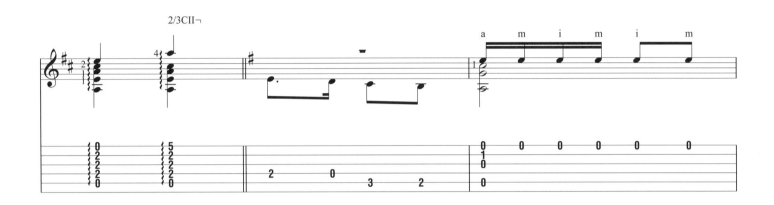

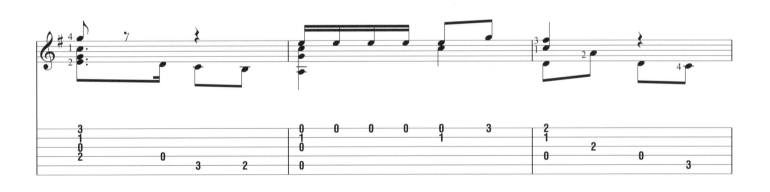

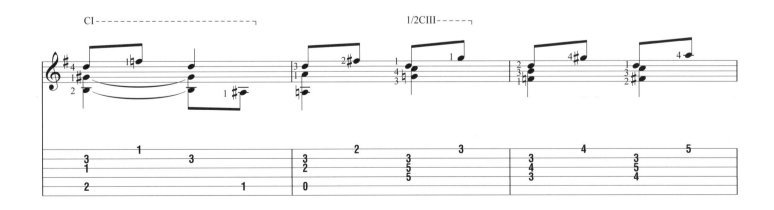

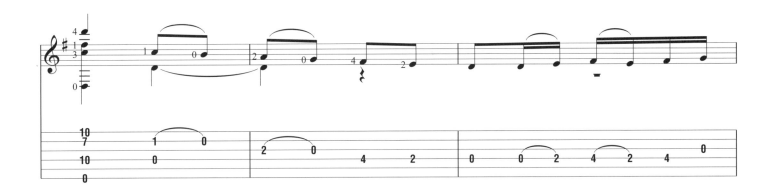

⊕ Coda

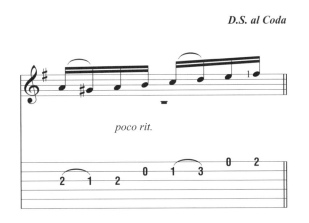

D.S. al Coda

poco rit.

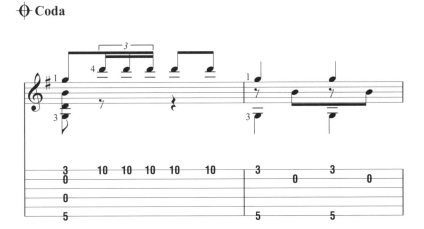

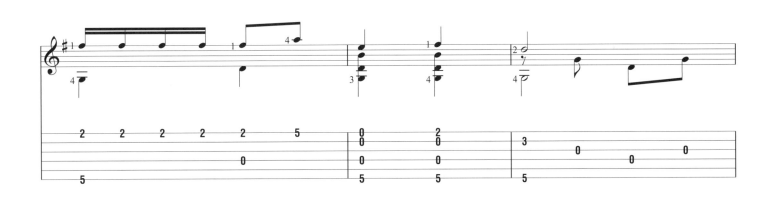

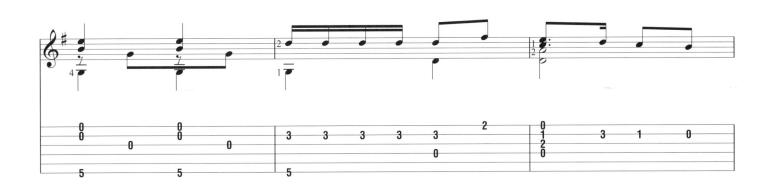

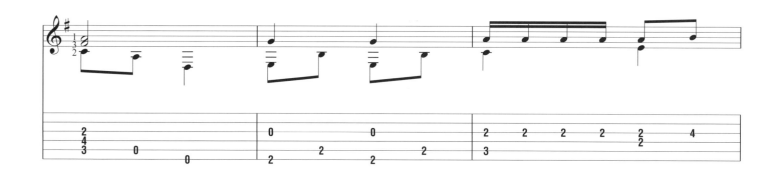

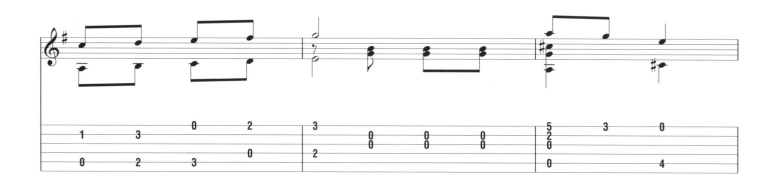

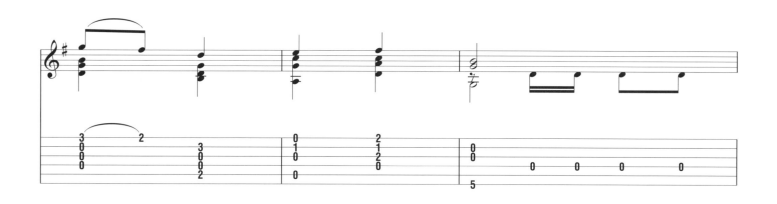

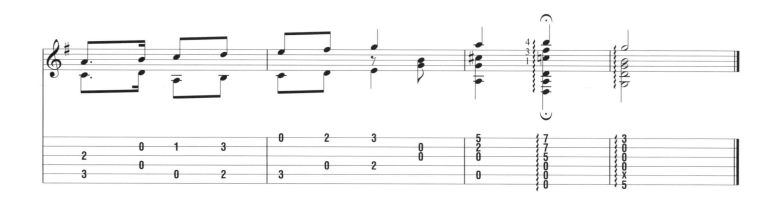

La Paloma Blanca
(The White Dove)

By S. Yradier

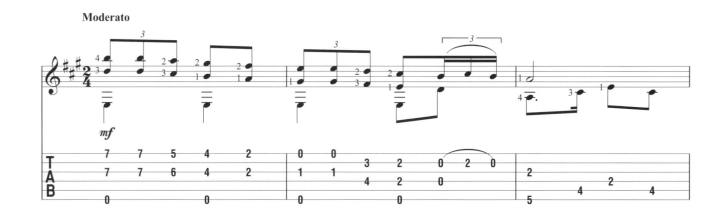

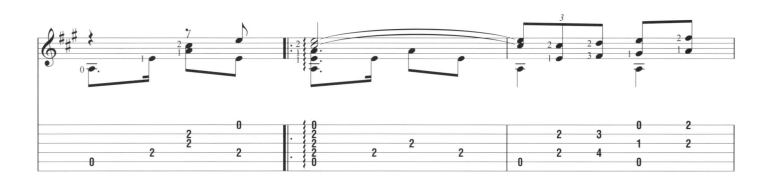

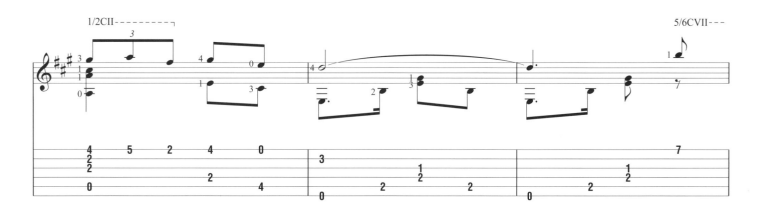

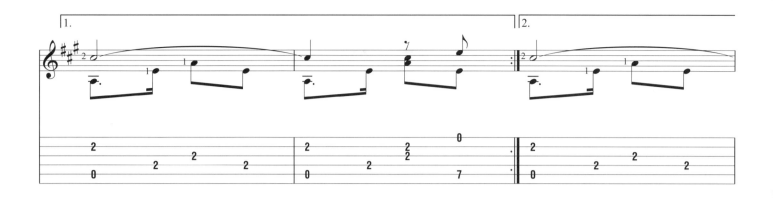

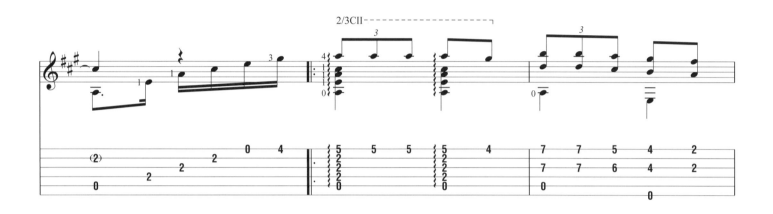

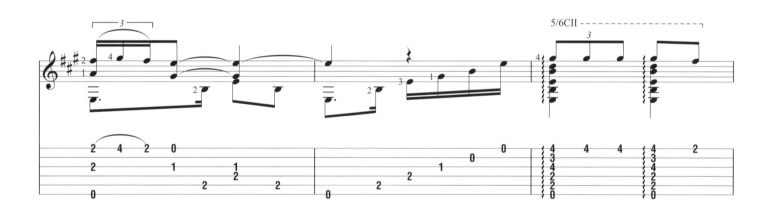

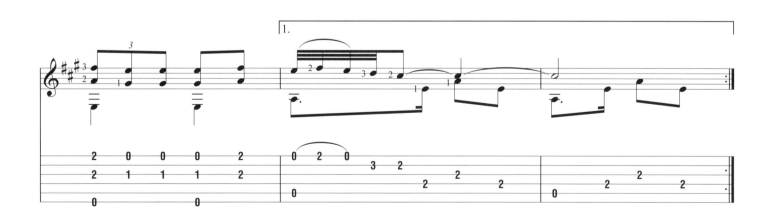

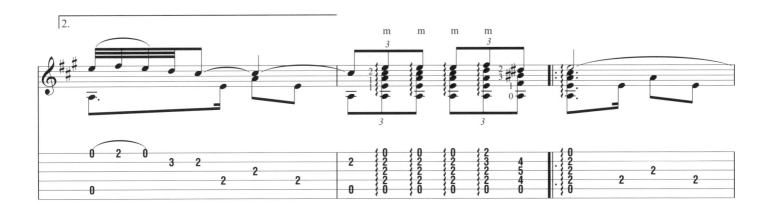

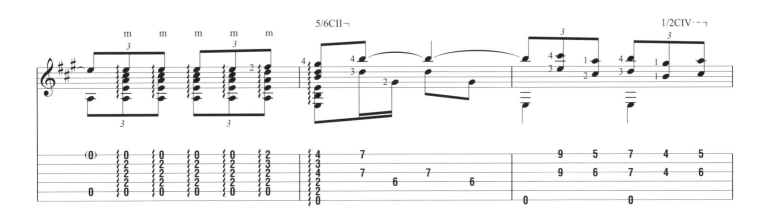

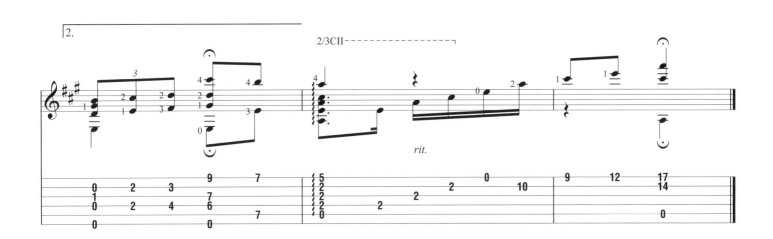

La Donna È Mobile

from RIGOLETTO
By Giuseppe Verdi

Tuning:
(low to high) D-A-D-G-B-E

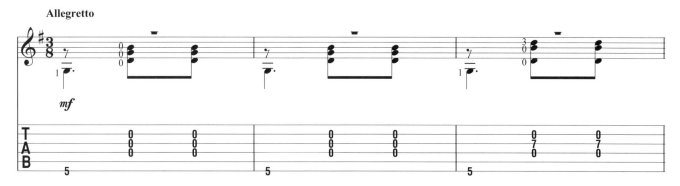

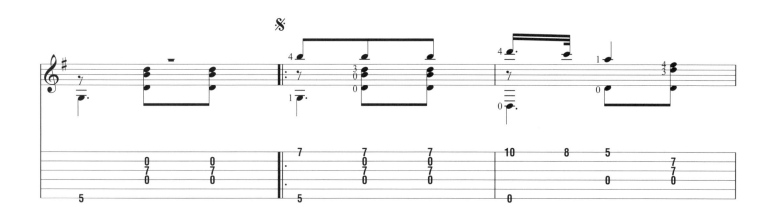

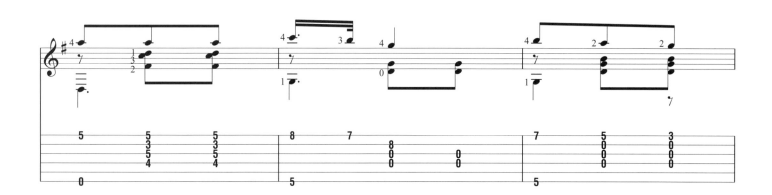

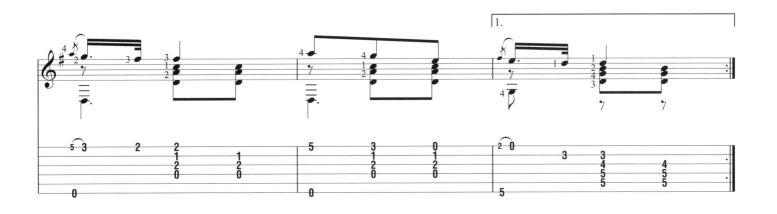

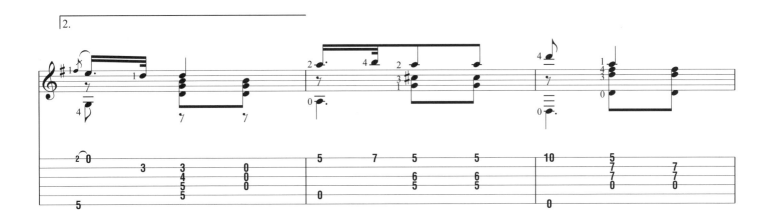

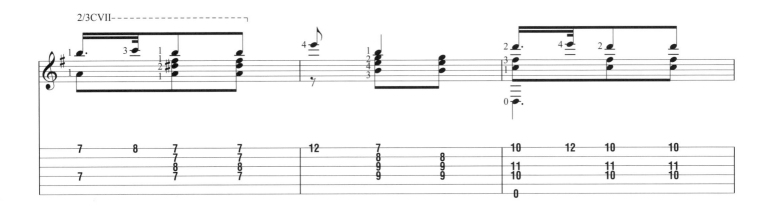

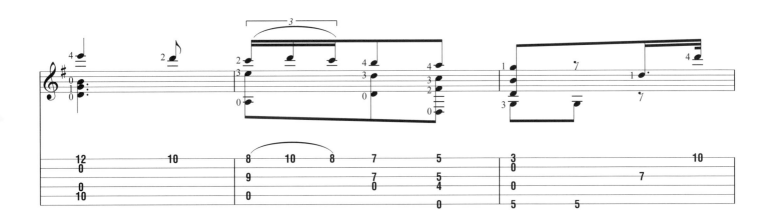

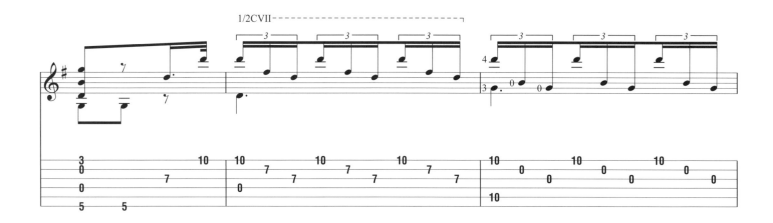

To Coda ⊕

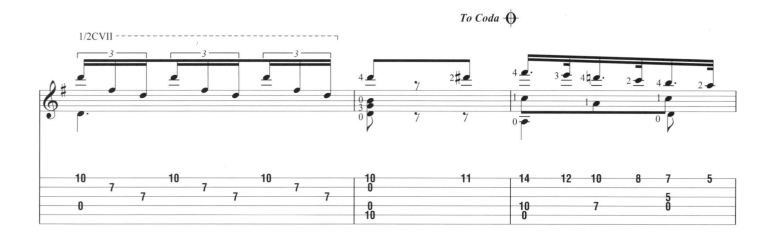

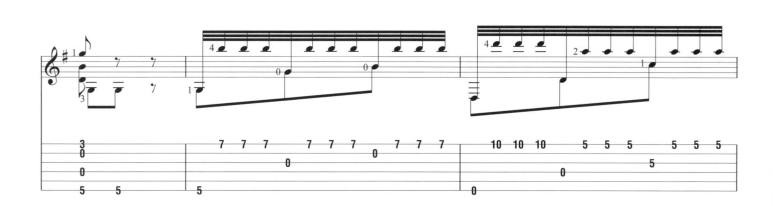

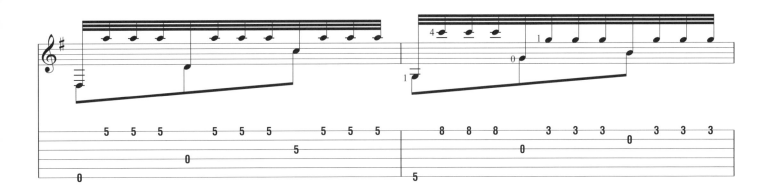

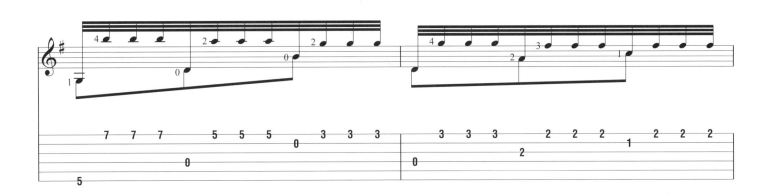

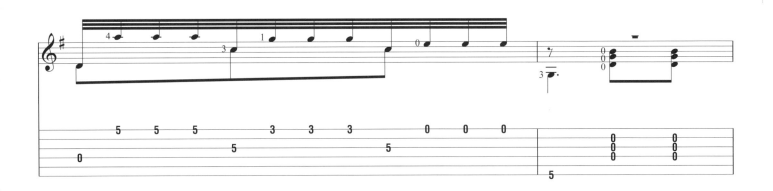

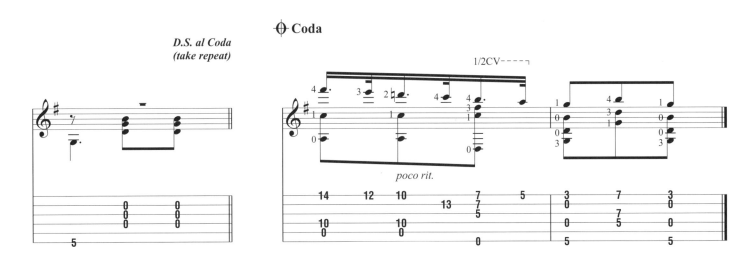

D.S. al Coda
(take repeat)

Coda

poco rit.

1/2CV- - - - ¬

Libiamo
(Brindisi)

from LA TRAVIATA (THE FALLEN WOMAN)
By Giuseppe Verdi

Tuning:
(low to high) D-A-D-G-B-E

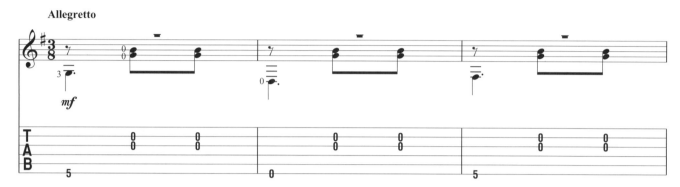

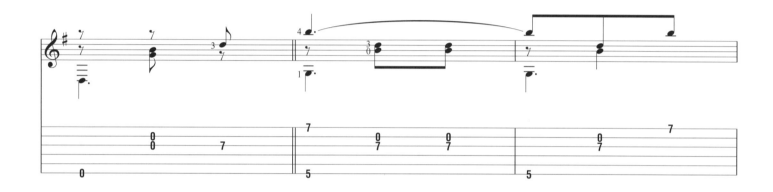

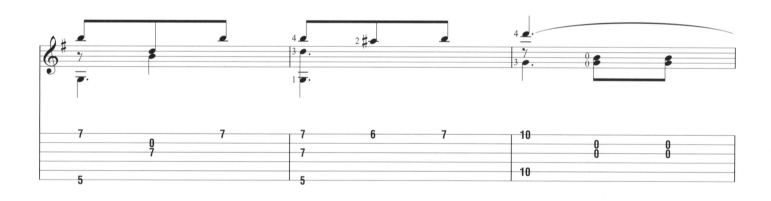

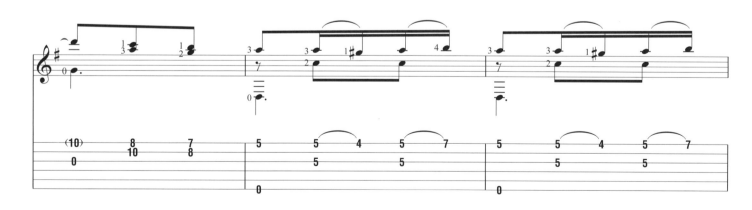

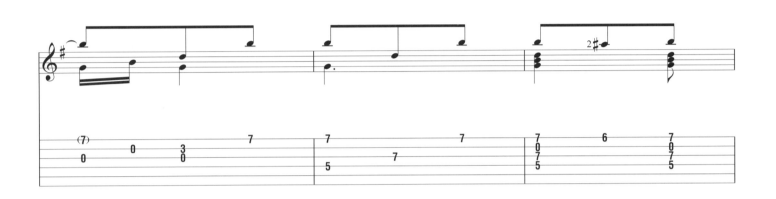

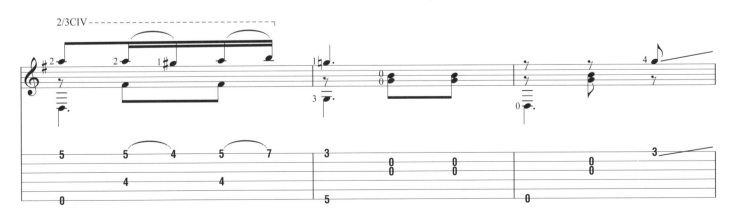

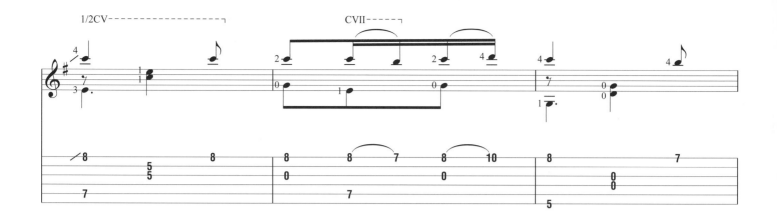

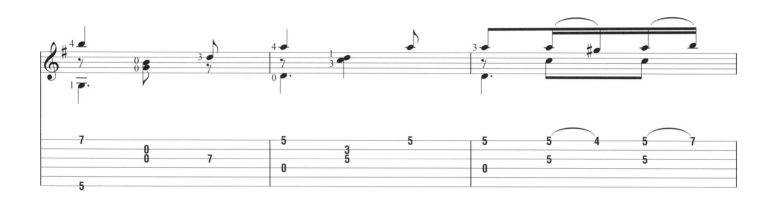

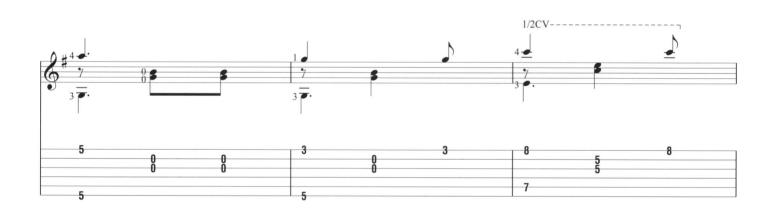

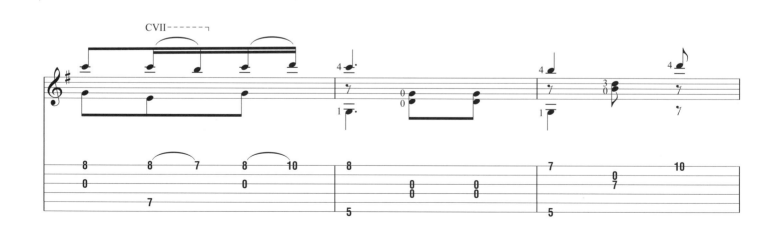

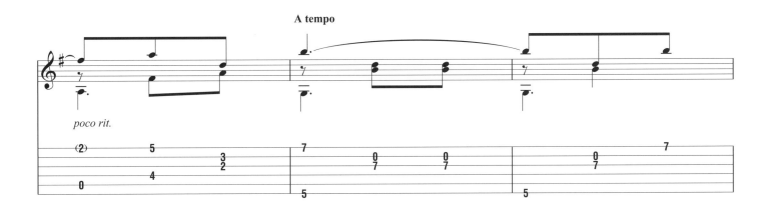

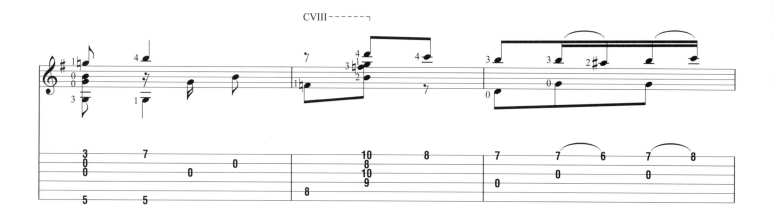

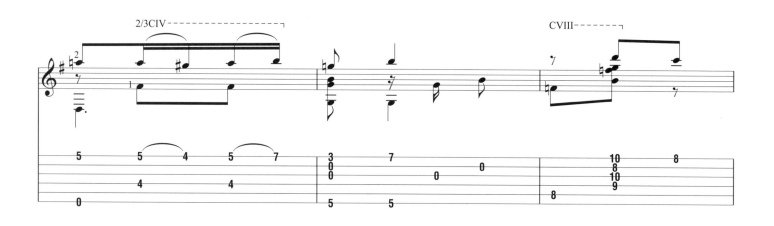

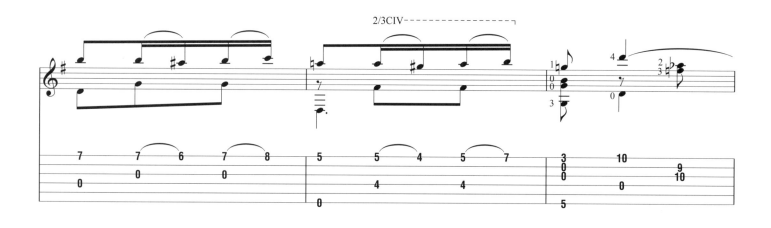

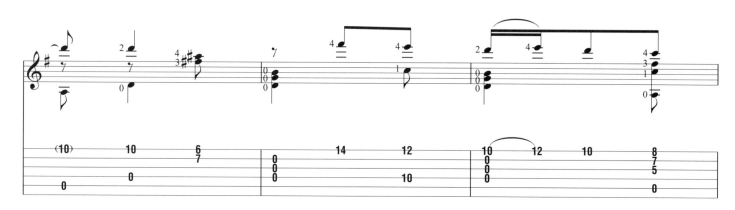

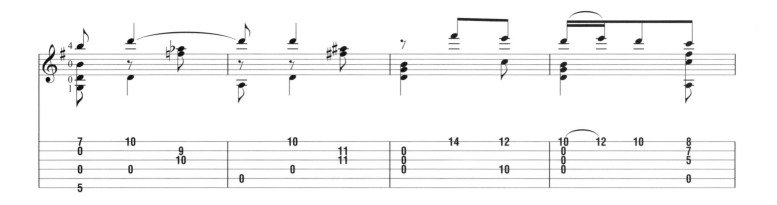

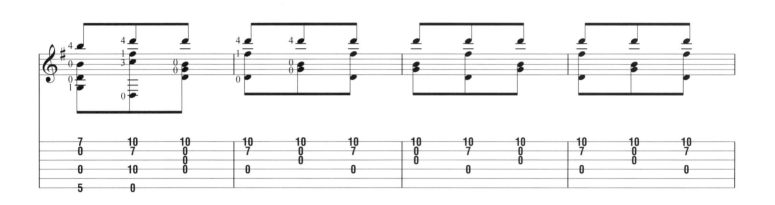

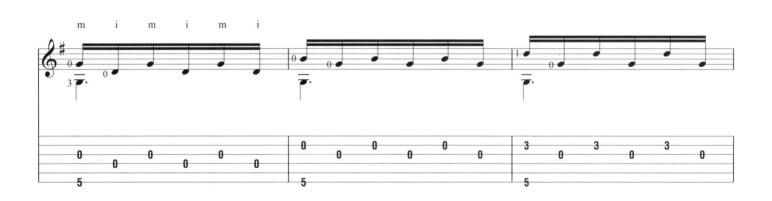

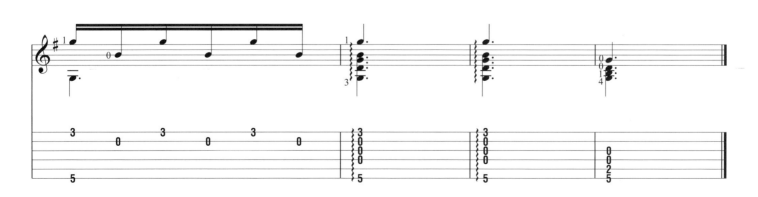

Mattinata

By Ruggero Leoncavallo

Allegretto

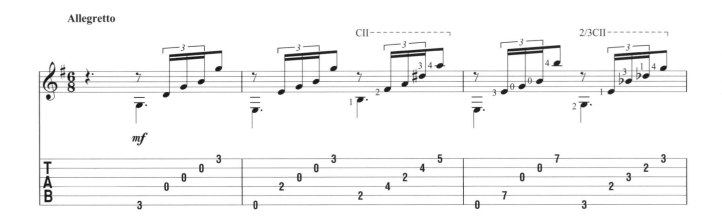

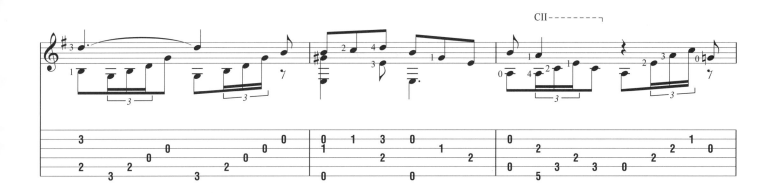

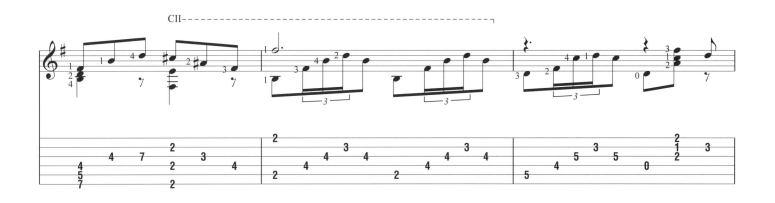

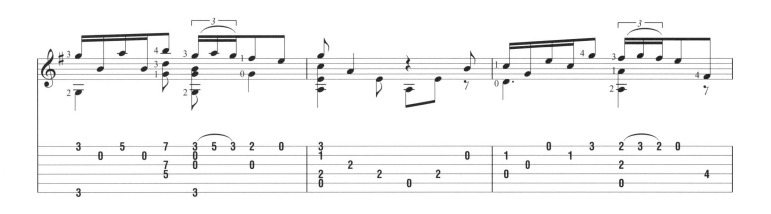

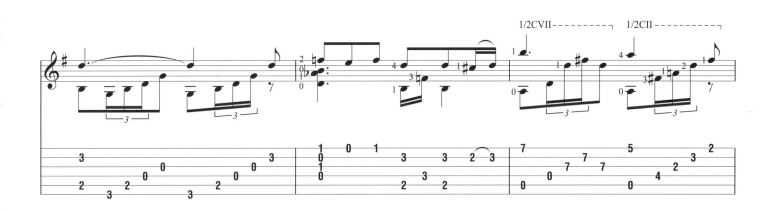

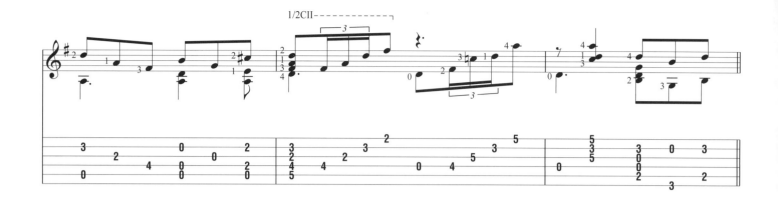

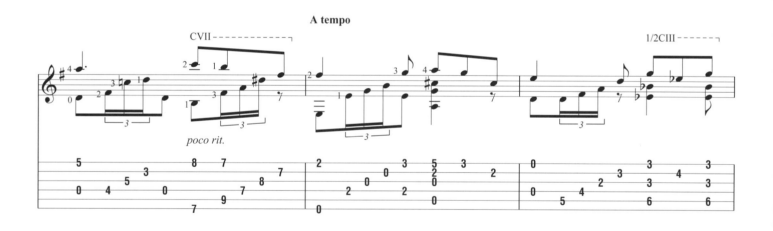

A tempo

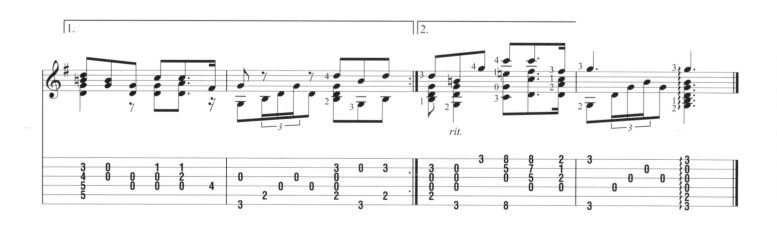

Musetta's Waltz
(Quando Men Vo)

from LA BOHÈME

Words by Giuseppe Giacosa and Luigi Illica
Music by Giacomo Puccini

Tuning:
(low to high) D-A-D-G-B-E

Moderato

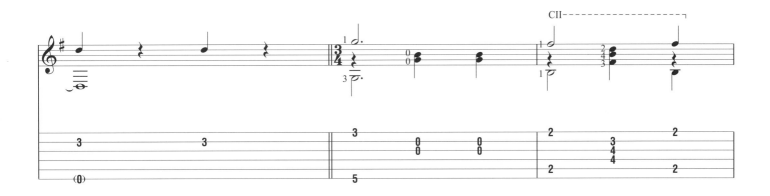

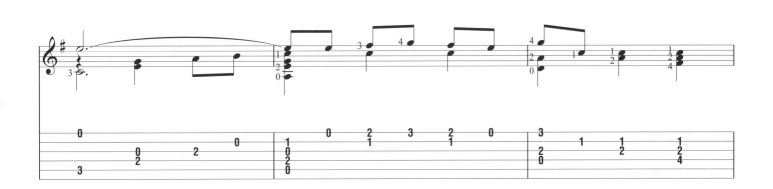

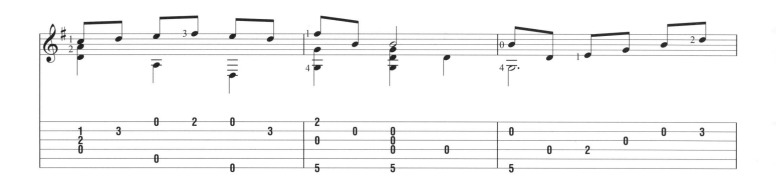

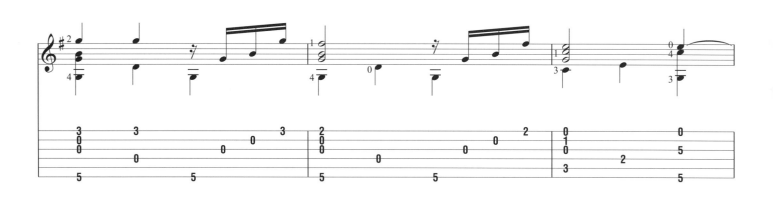

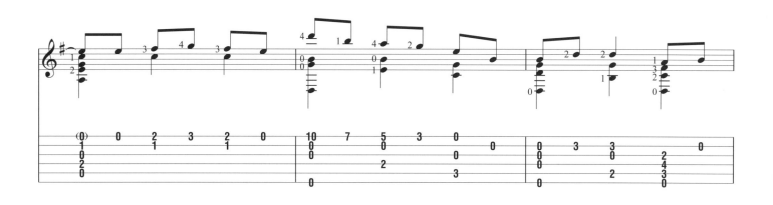

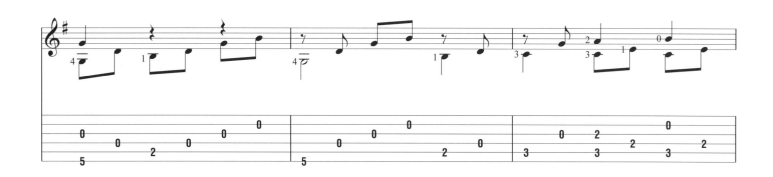

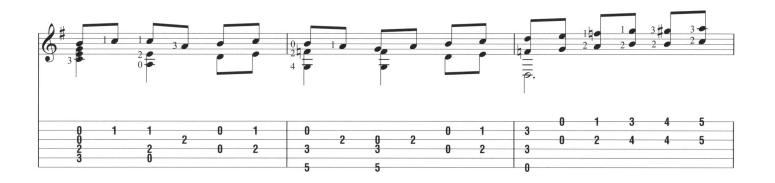

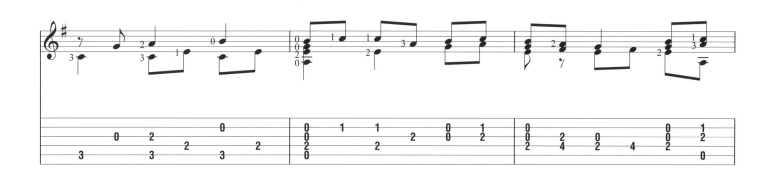

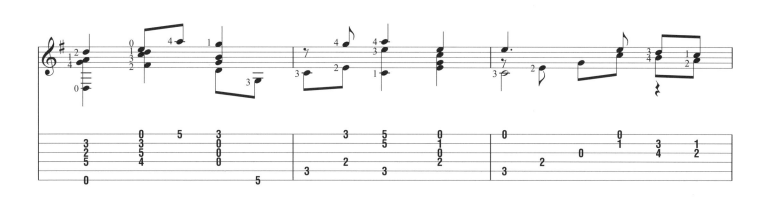

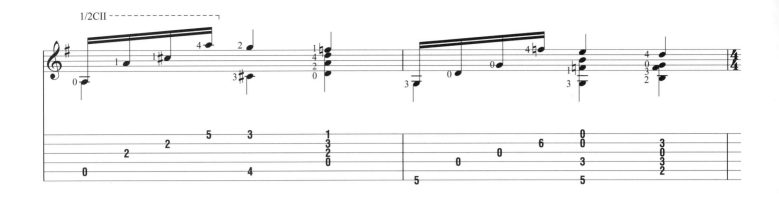

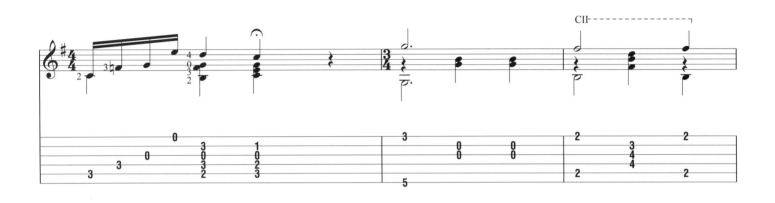

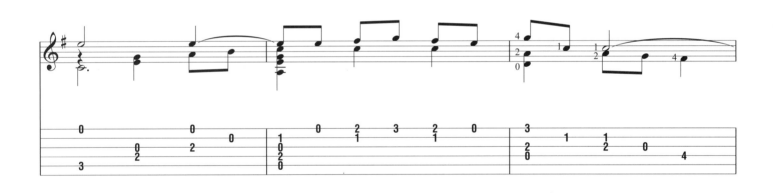

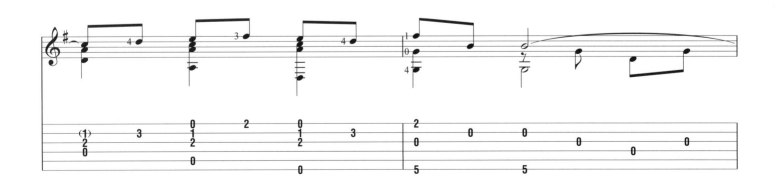

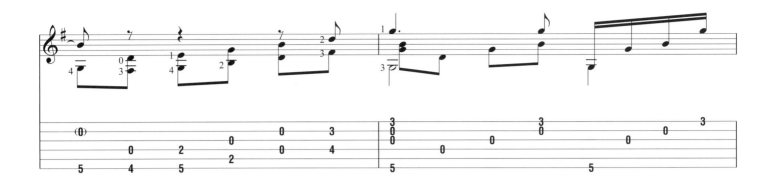

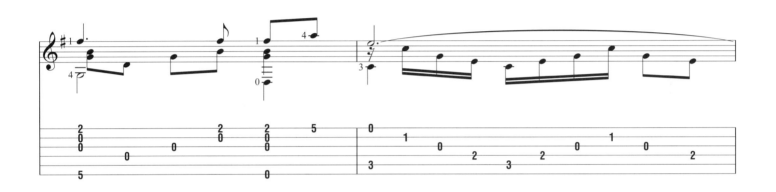

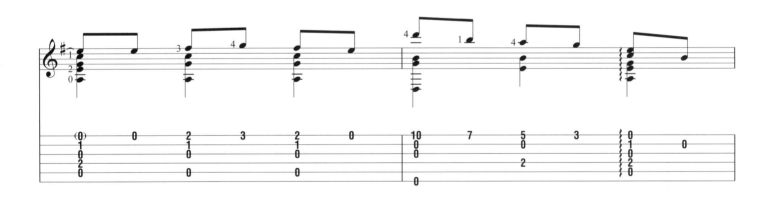

O Mio Babbino Caro

from GIANNI SCHICCHI
By Giacomo Puccini

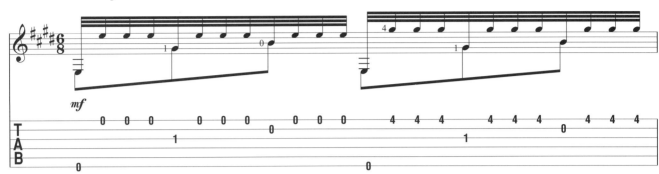

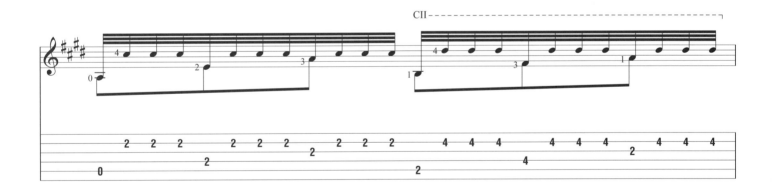

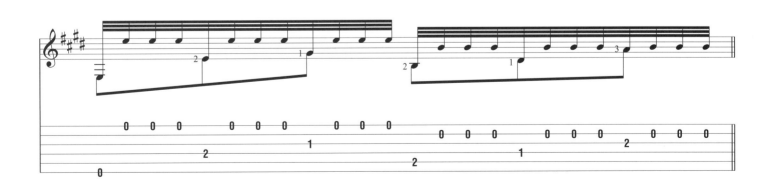

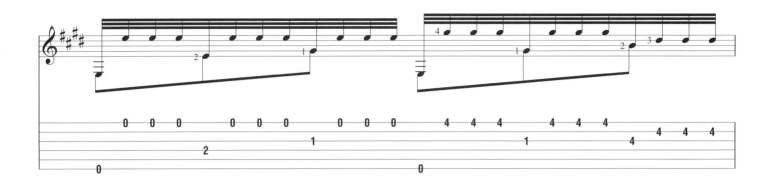

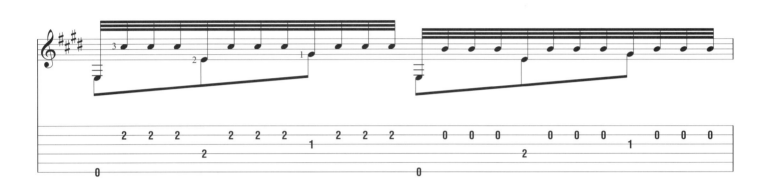

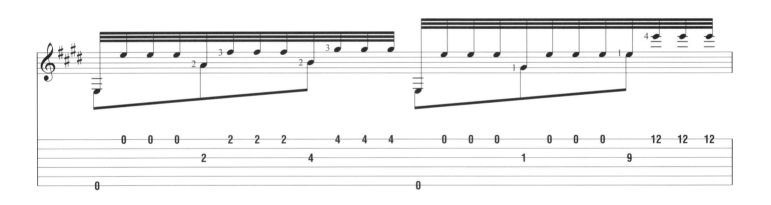

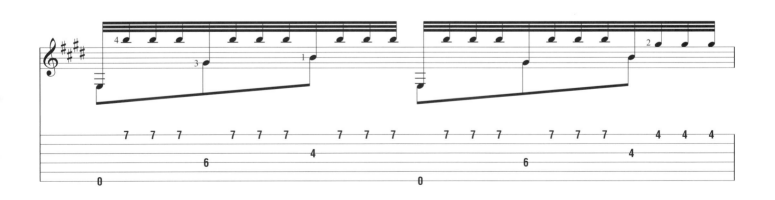

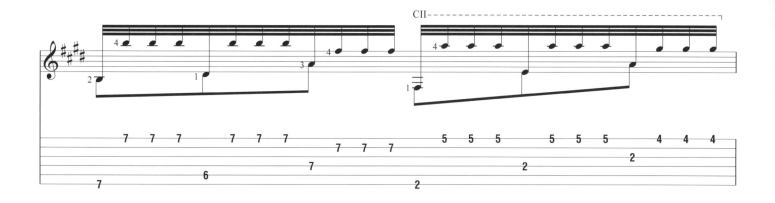

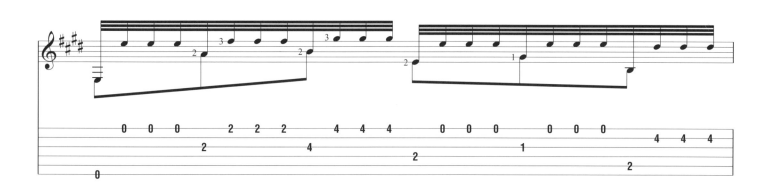

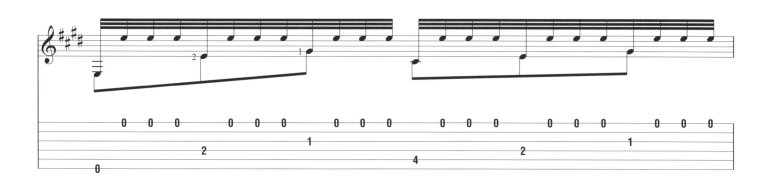

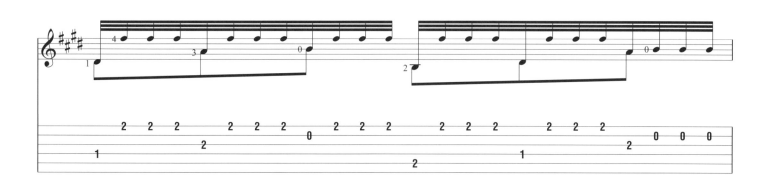

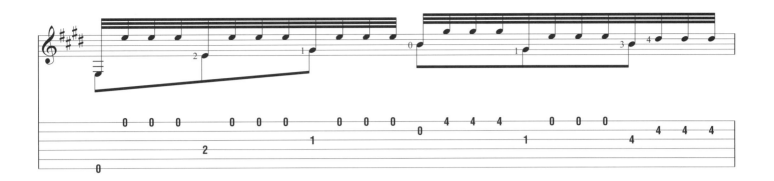

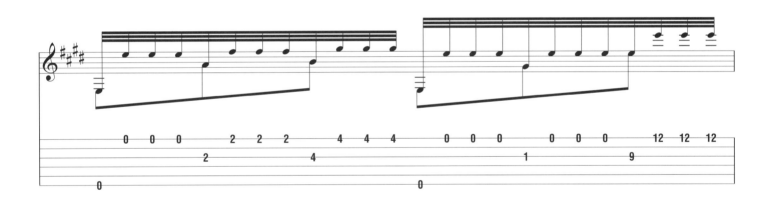

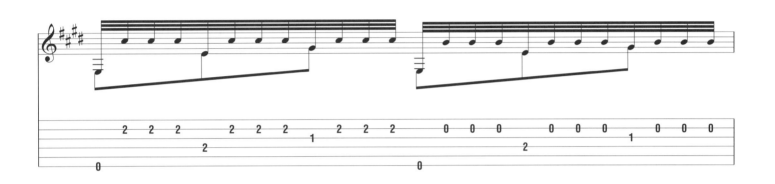

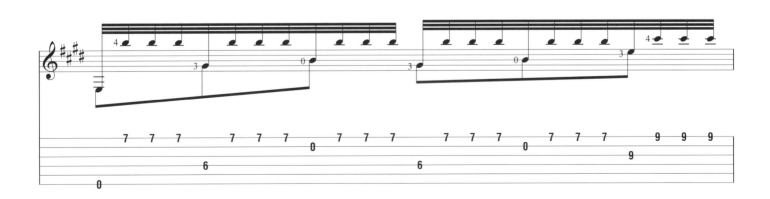

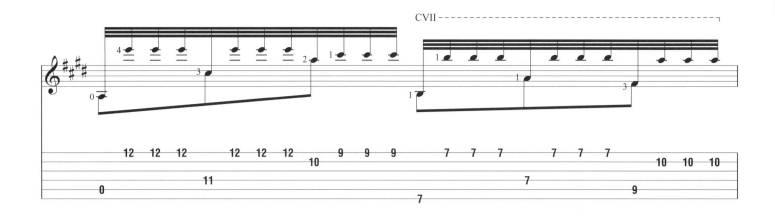

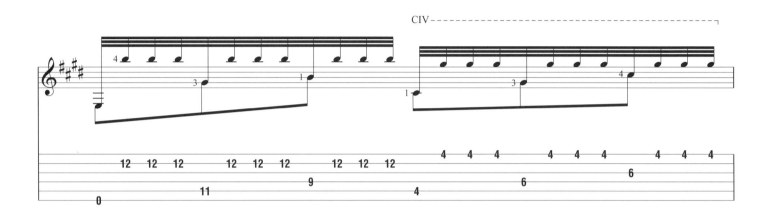

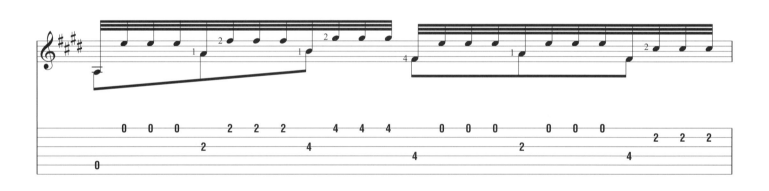

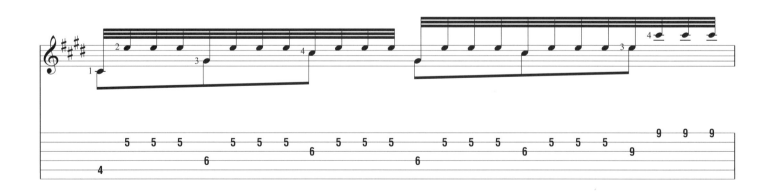

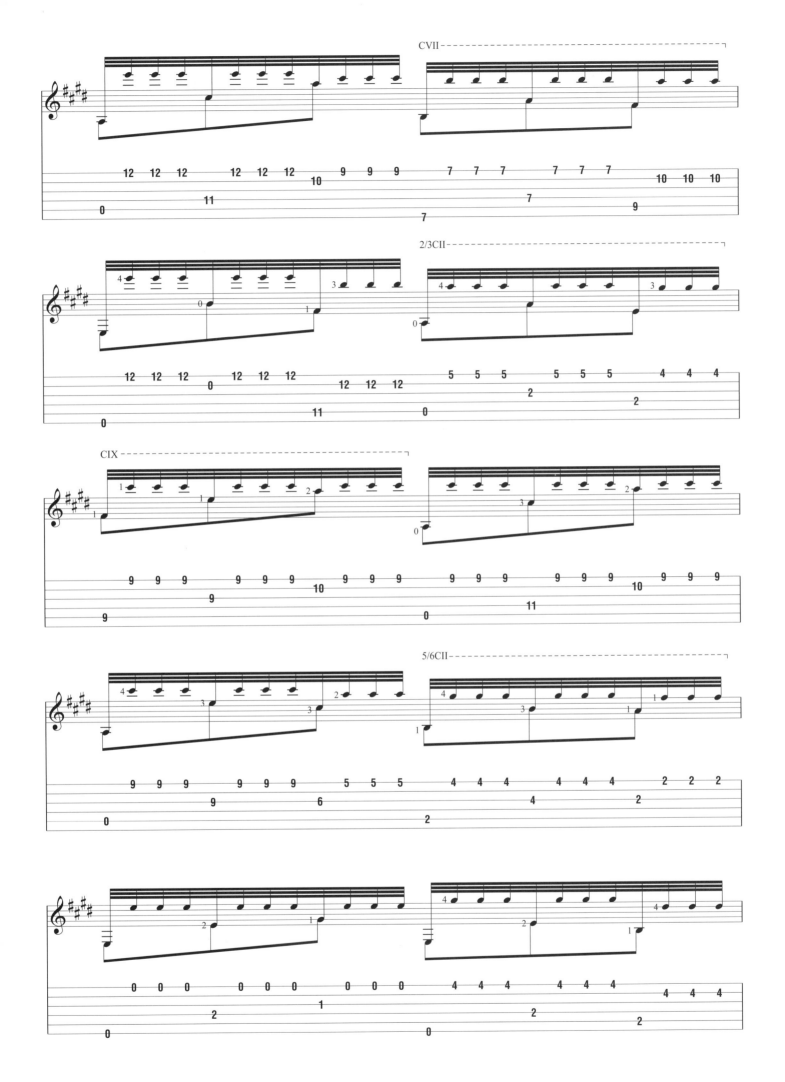

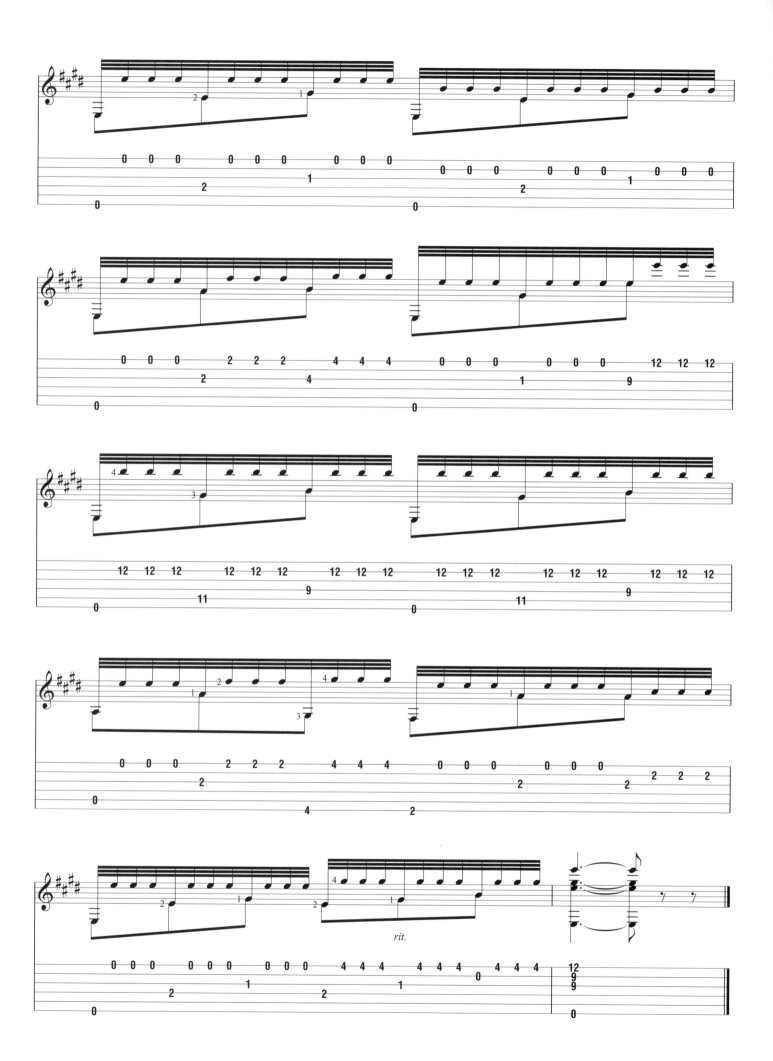

Oh Marie

Words and Music by Eduardo di Capua

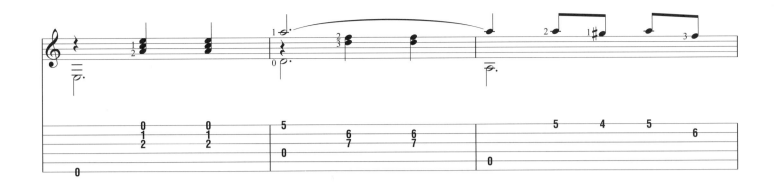

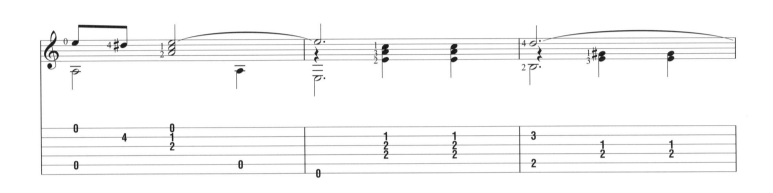

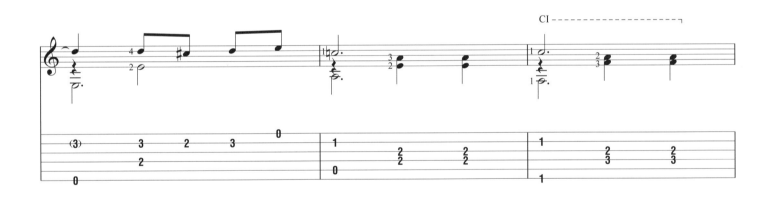

82

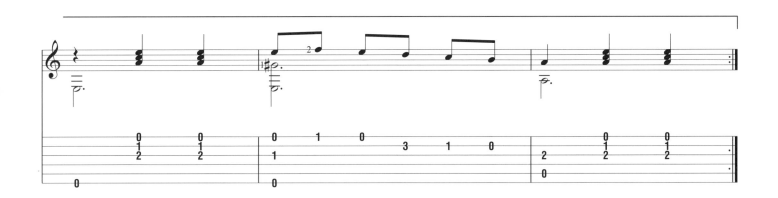

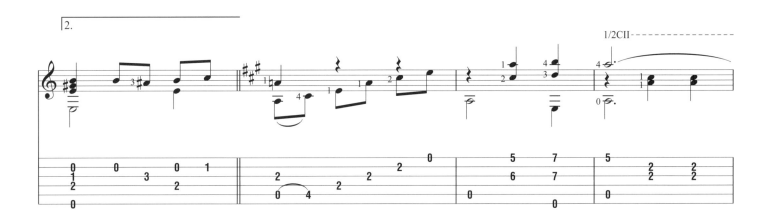

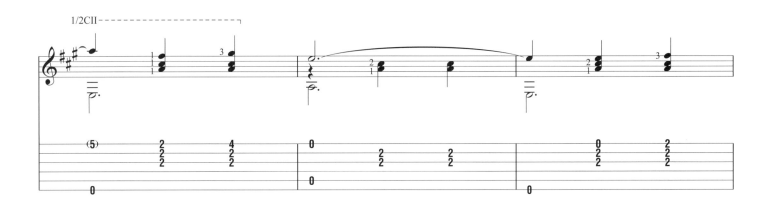

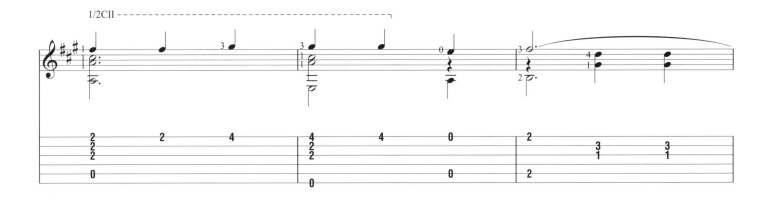

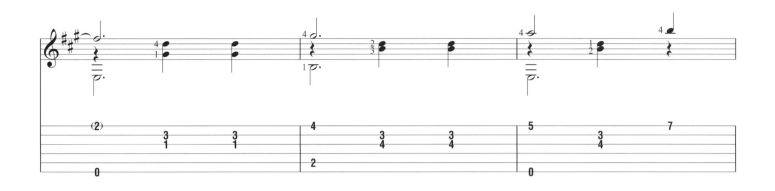

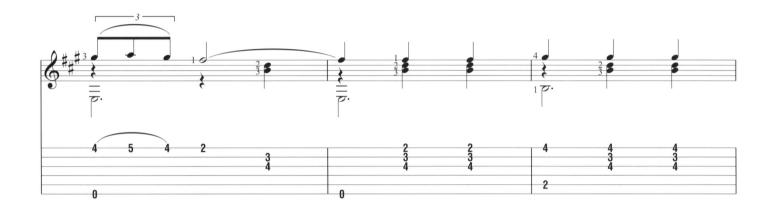

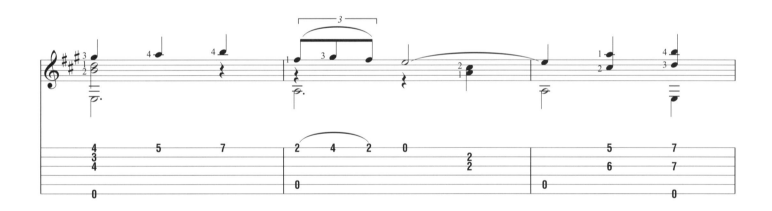

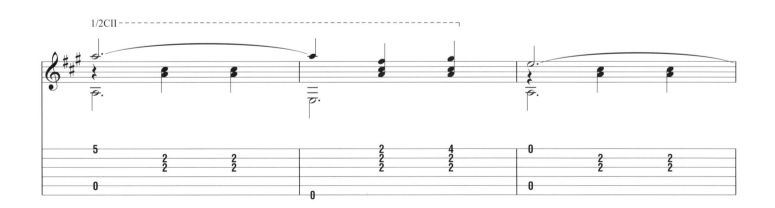

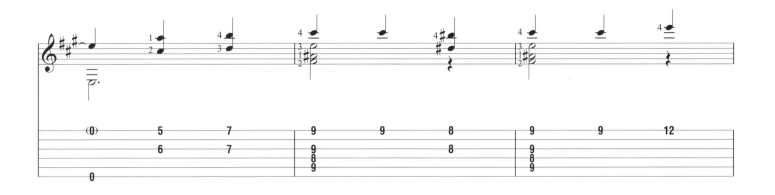

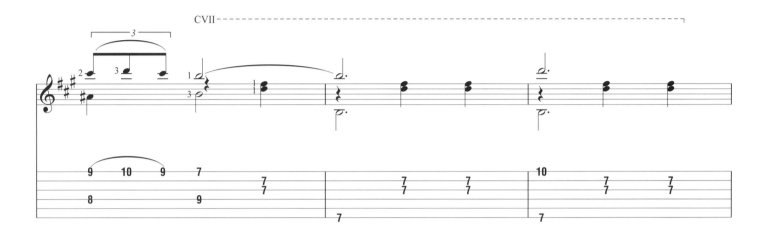

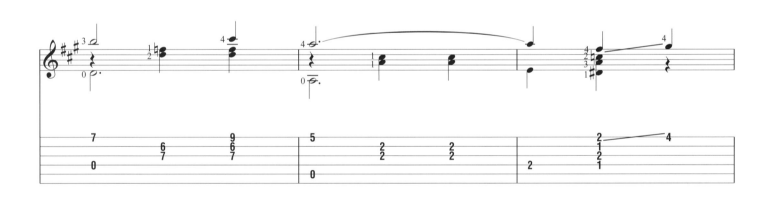

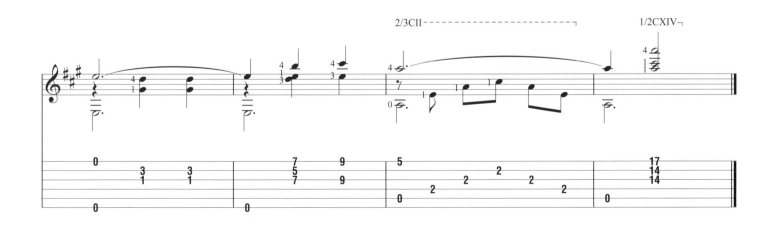

'O Sole Mio

Words by Giovanni Capurro
Music by Eduardo di Capua

Tuning:
(low to high) D-A-D-G-B-E

Andante espressivo

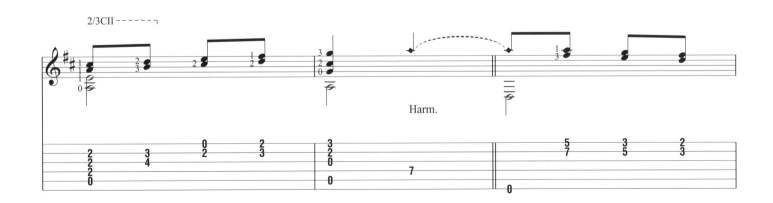

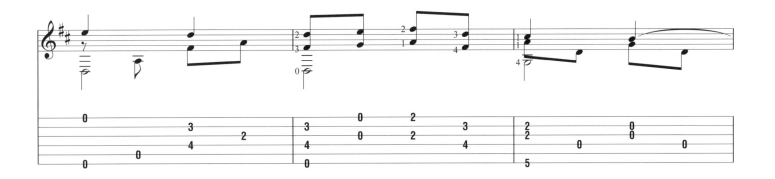

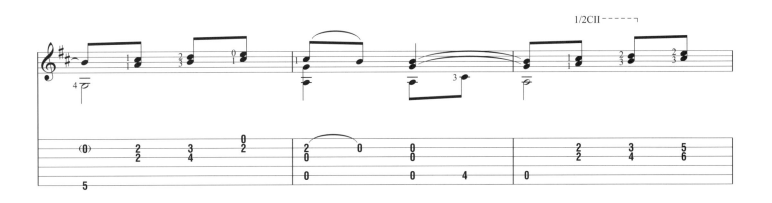

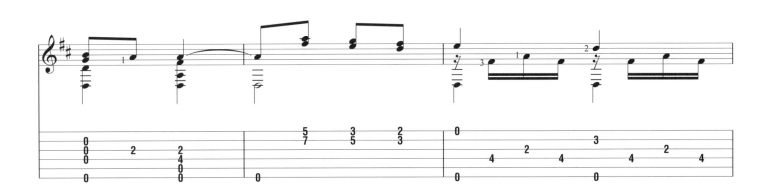

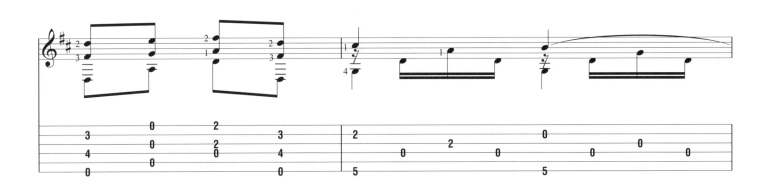

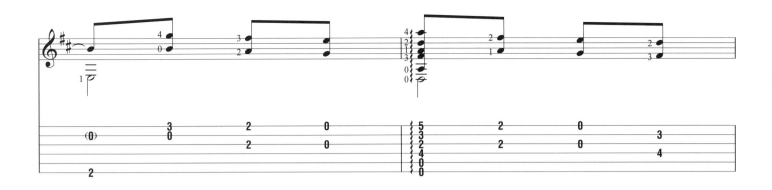

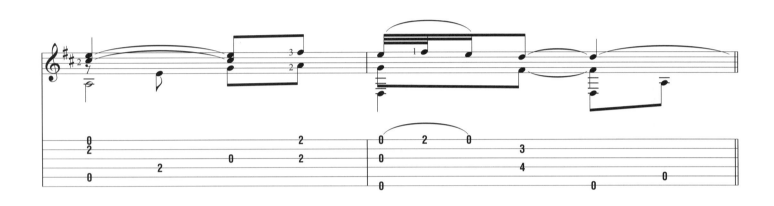

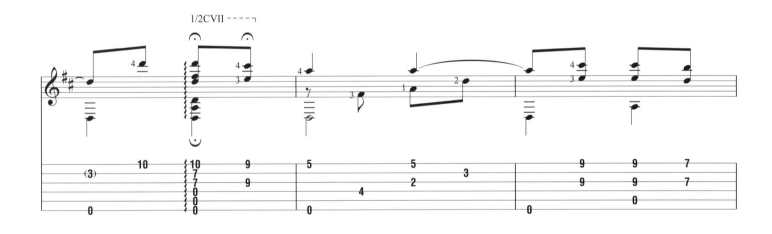

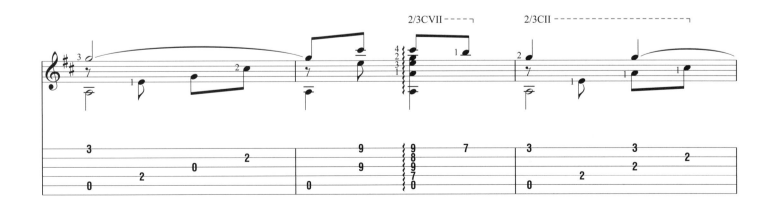

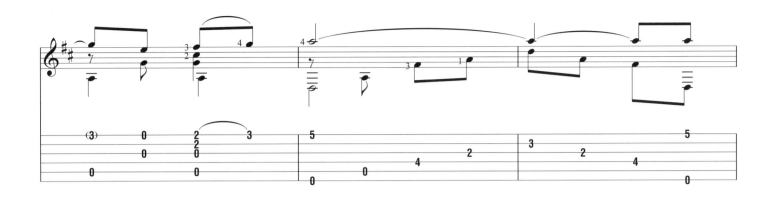

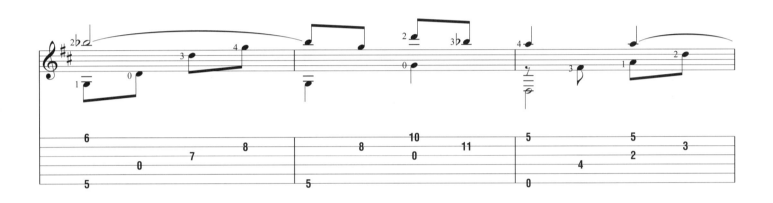

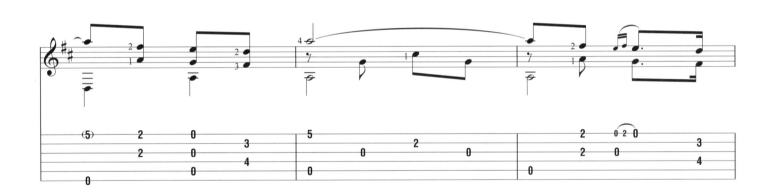

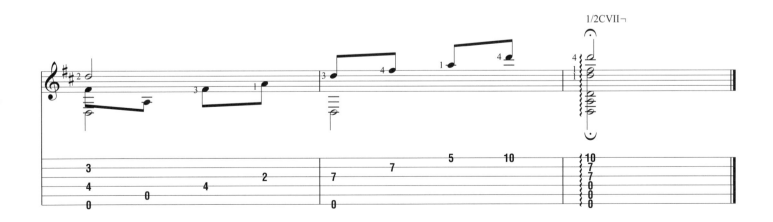

Santa Lucia

By Teodoro Cottrau

Valse andantino

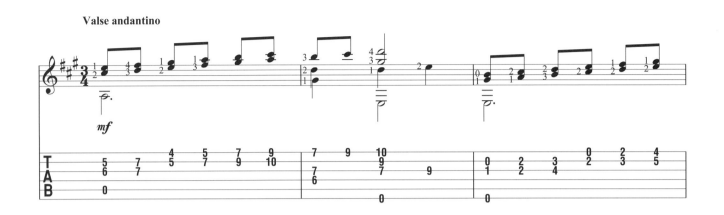

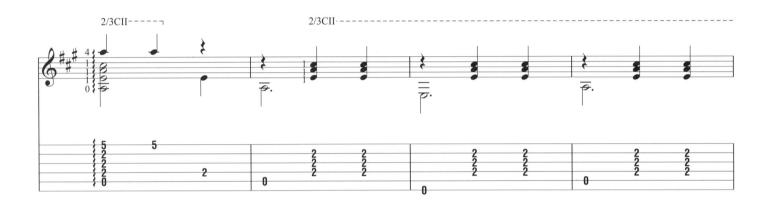

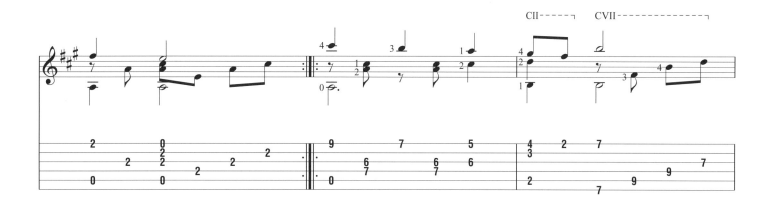

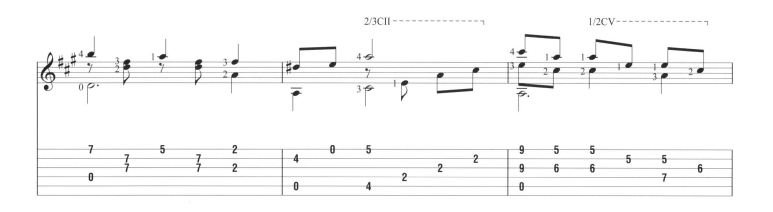

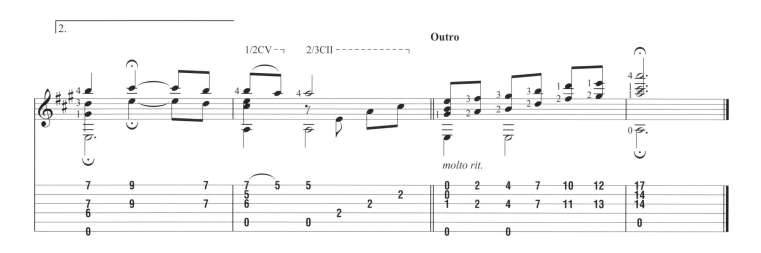

Tarantella

Traditional

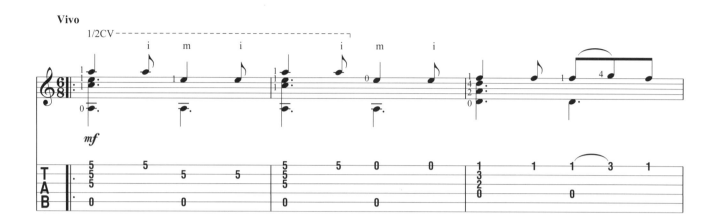

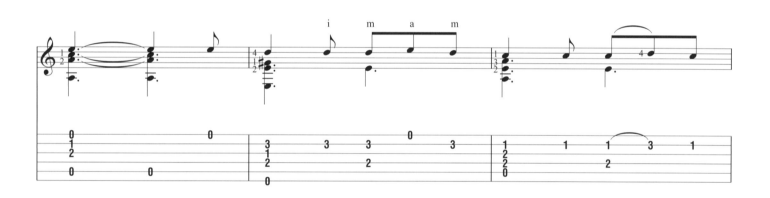

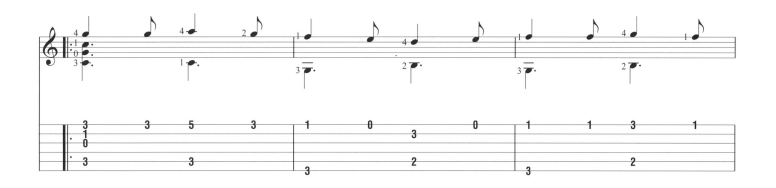

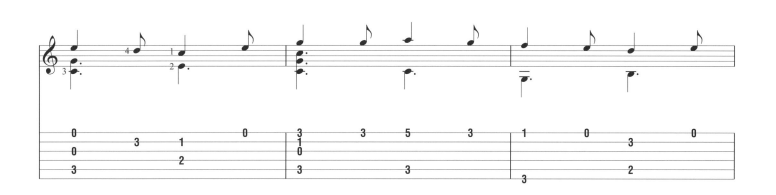

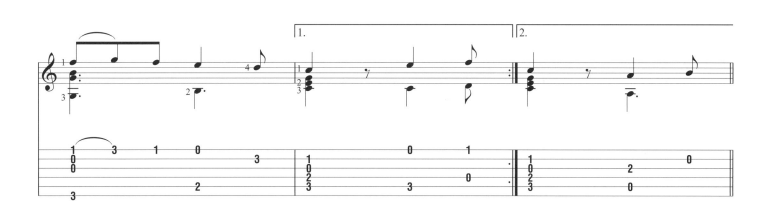

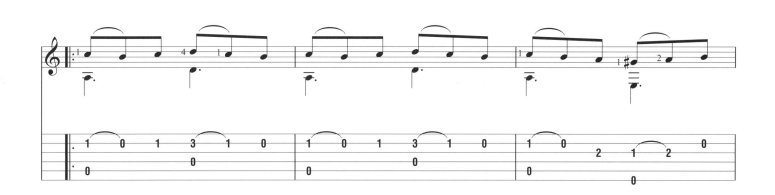

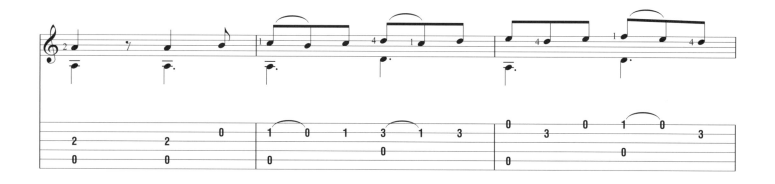

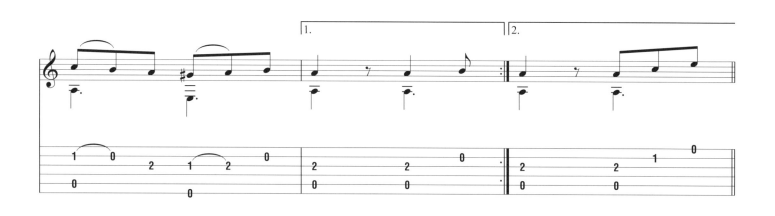

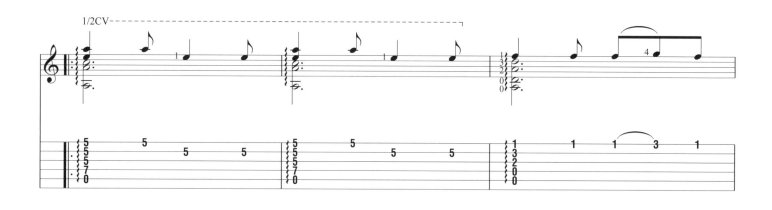

To Coda ⊕

⊕ **Coda**

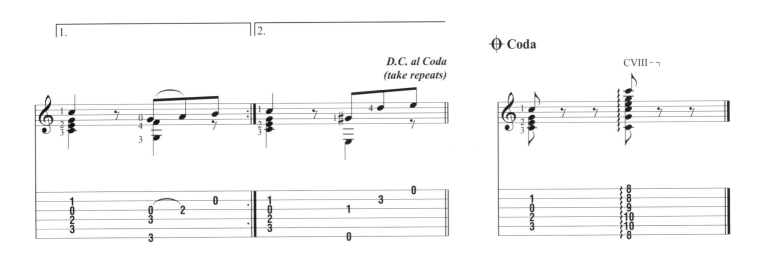

Serenata

By Enrico Toselli

Moderato espressivo

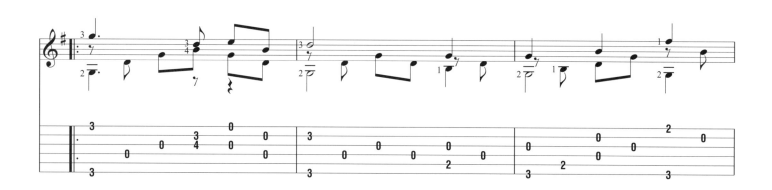

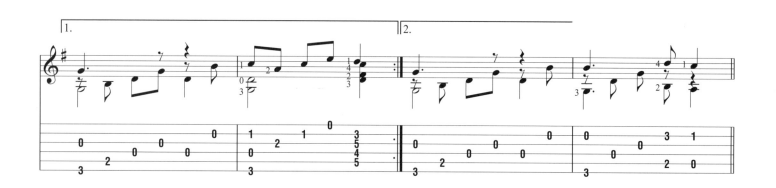

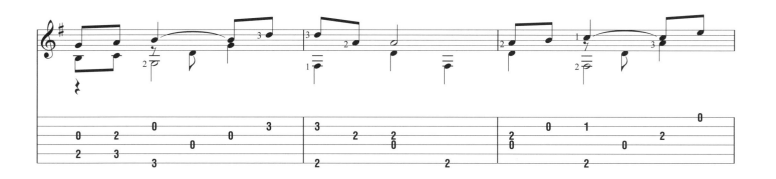

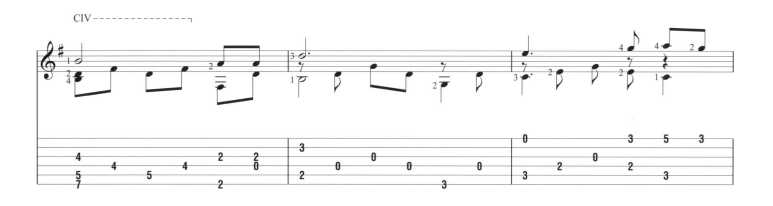

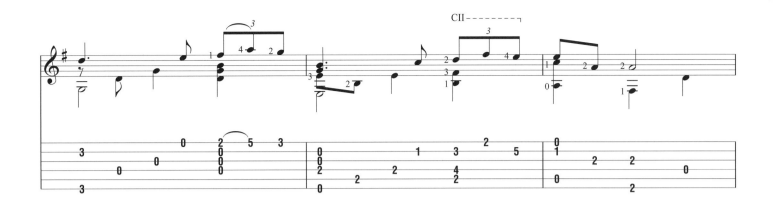

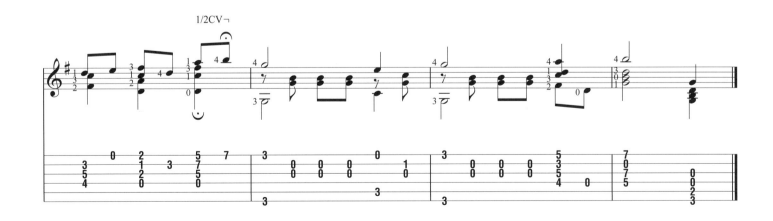

Vieni Sul Mar

Italian Folk Song

Tuning:
(low to high) D-A-D-G-B-E

Moderato

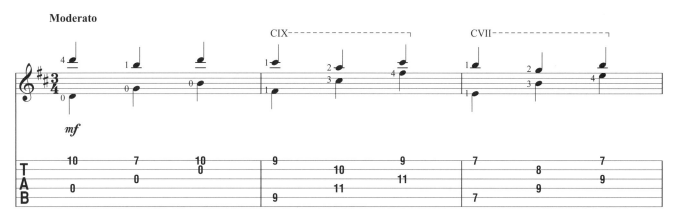

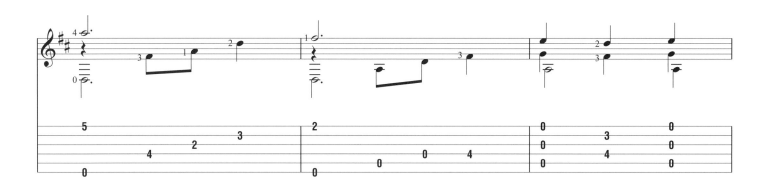

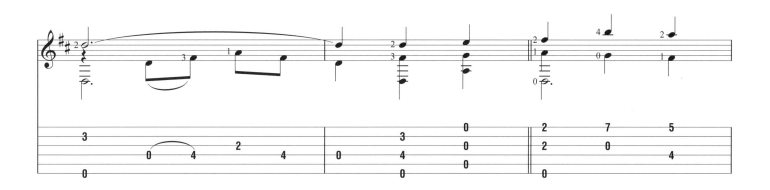

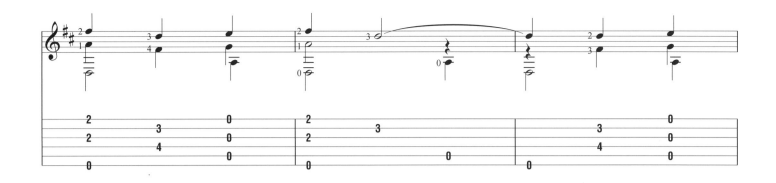

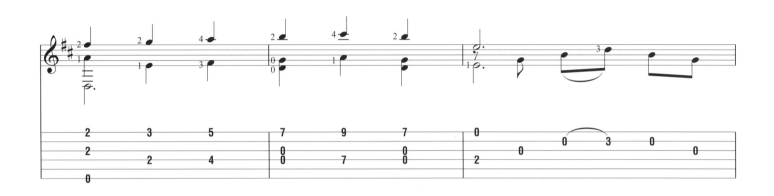

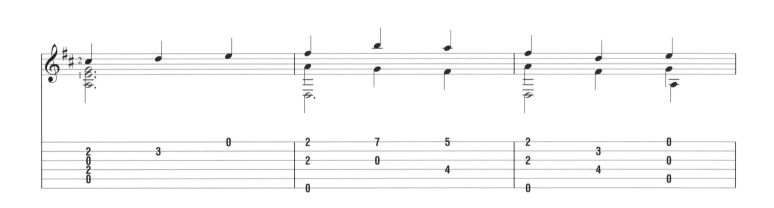

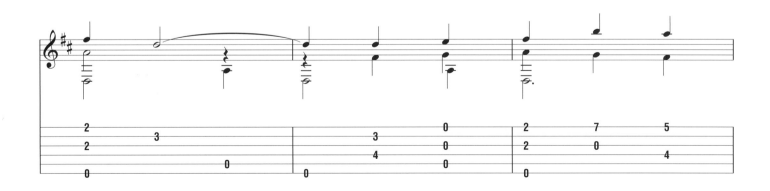

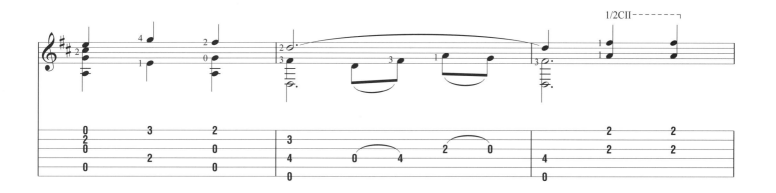

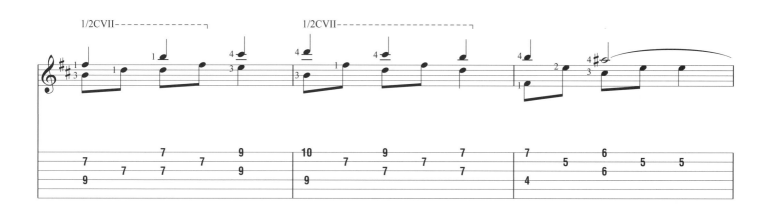

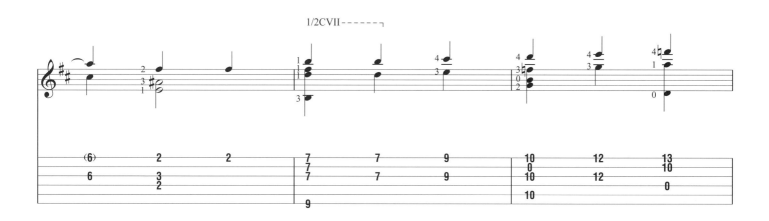

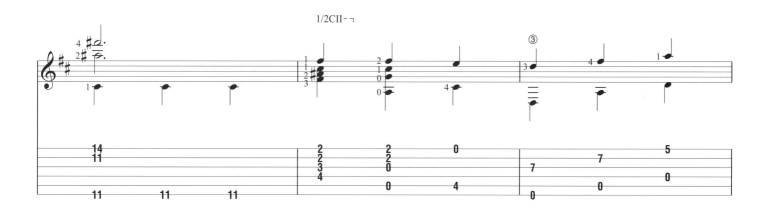

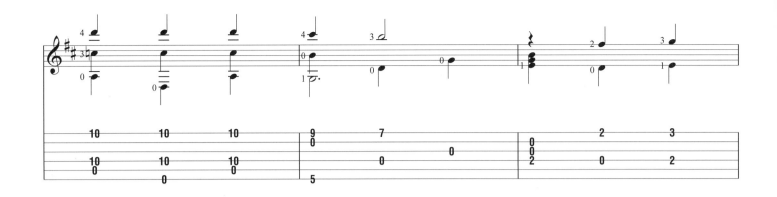

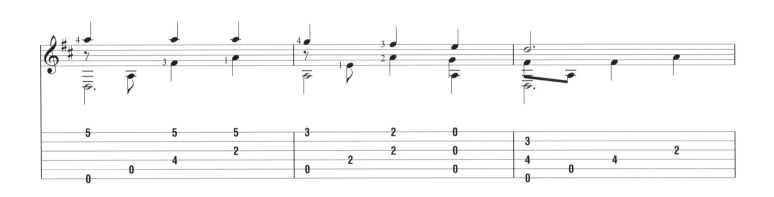

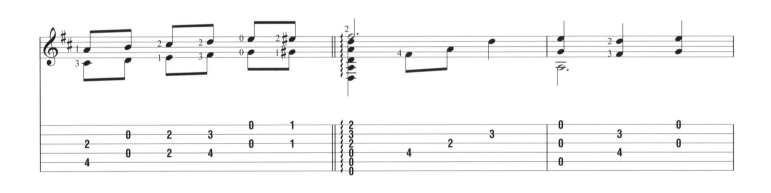

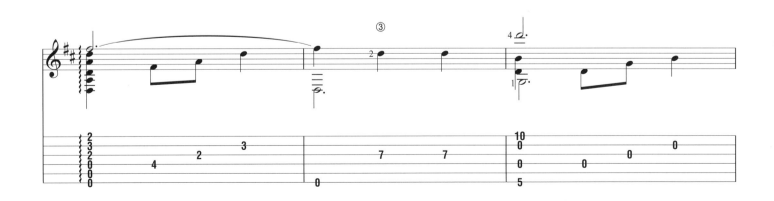

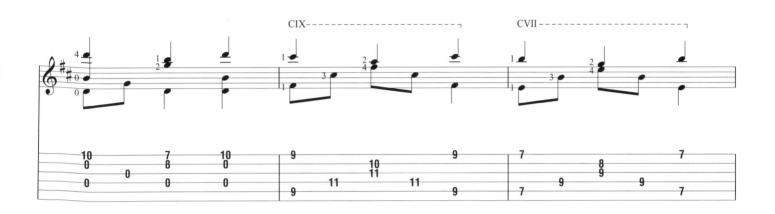

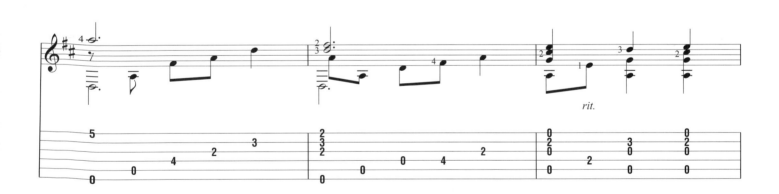

CLASSICAL GUITAR PUBLICATIONS FROM HAL LEONARD

THE BEATLES FOR CLASSICAL GUITAR

Includes 20 solos from big Beatles hits arranged for classical guitar, complete with left-hand and right-hand fingering. Songs include: All My Loving • And I Love Her • Can't Buy Me Love • Fool on the Hill • From a Window • Hey Jude • If I Fell • Let It Be • Michelle • Norwegian Wood • Obla Di • Ticket to Ride • Yesterday • and more. Features arrangements and an introduction by Joe Washington, as well as his helpful hints on classical technique and detailed notes on how to play each song. The book also covers parts and specifications of the classical guitar, tuning, and Joe's "Strata System" – an easy-reading system applied to chord diagrams.

_____ 00699237 Classical Guitar.....................$19.99

MATTEO CARCASSI – 25 MELODIC AND PROGRESSIVE STUDIES, OP. 60
arr. Paul Henry

One of Carcassi's (1792-1853) most famous collections of classical guitar music – indispensable for the modern guitarist's musical and technical development. Performed by Paul Henry. 49-minute audio accompaniment.

_____ 00696506 Book/CD Pack.....................$17.95

CLASSICAL & FINGERSTYLE GUITAR TECHNIQUES
INCLUDES TAB

by David Oakes • Musicians Institute

This Master Class with MI instructor David Oakes is aimed at any electric or acoustic guitarist who wants a quick, thorough grounding in the essentials of classical and fingerstyle technique. Topics covered include: arpeggios and scales, free stroke and rest stroke, P-i scale technique, three-to-a-string patterns, natural and artificial harmonics, tremolo and rasgueado, and more. The book includes 12 intensive lessons for right and left hand in standard notation & tab, and the CD features 92 solo acoustic tracks.

_____ 00695171 Book/CD Pack.....................$17.99

CLASSICAL GUITAR CHRISTMAS COLLECTION
INCLUDES TAB

Includes classical guitar arrangements in standard notation and tablature for more than two dozen beloved carols: Angels We Have Heard on High • Auld Lang Syne • Ave Maria • Away in a Manger • Canon in D • The First Noel • God Rest Ye Merry, Gentlemen • Hark! the Herald Angels Sing • I Saw Three Ships • Jesu, Joy of Man's Desiring • Joy to the World • O Christmas Tree • O Holy Night • Silent Night • What Child Is This? • and more.

_____ 00699493 Guitar Solo $9.95

CLASSICAL GUITAR WEDDING
INCLUDES TAB

Perfect for players hired to perform for someone's big day, this songbook features 16 classical wedding favorites arranged for solo guitar in standard notation and tablature. Includes: Air on the G String • Ave Maria • Bridal Chorus • Canon in D • Jesu, Joy of Man's Desiring • Minuet • Sheep May Safely Graze • Wedding March • and more.

_____ 00699563 Solo Guitar with Tab $10.95

CLASSICAL MASTERPIECES FOR GUITAR
INCLUDES TAB

27 works by Bach, Beethoven, Handel, Mendelssohn, Mozart and more transcribed with standard notation and tablature. Now anyone can enjoy classical material regardless of their guitar background. Also features stay-open binding.

_____ 00699312 ....$12.95

CLASSICAL THEMES
INCLUDES TAB

20 beloved classical themes arranged for easy guitar in large-size notes (with the note names in the note heads) and tablature. Includes: Air on the G String (Bach) • Ave Maria (Schubert) • Für Elise (Beethoven) • In the Hall of the Mountain King (Grieg) • Jesu, Joy of Man's Desiring (Bach) • Largo (Handel) • Ode to Joy (Beethoven) • Pomp and Circumstance (Elgar) • and more. Ideal for beginning or vision-impaired players.

_____ 00699272 E-Z Play Guitar........................$9.95

MASTERWORKS FOR GUITAR
INCLUDES TAB

Over 60 Favorites from Four Centuries
World's Great Classical Music

Dozens of classical masterpieces: Allemande • Bourree • Canon in D • Jesu, Joy of Man's Desiring • Lagrima • Malaguena • Mazurka • Piano Sonata No. 14 in C# Minor (Moonlight) Op. 27 No. 2 First Movement Theme • Ode to Joy • Prelude No. I (Well-Tempered Clavier).

_____ 00699503 ....$16.95

Visit Hal Leonard Online at **www.halleonard.com**

A MODERN APPROACH TO CLASSICAL GUITAR

by Charles Duncan

This multi-volume method was developed to allow students to study the art of classical guitar within a new, more contemporary framework. For private, class or self-instruction. Book One incorporates chord frames and symbols, as well as a recording to assist in tuning and to provide accompaniments for at-home practice. Book One also introduces beginning fingerboard technique and music theory. Book Two and Three build upon the techniques learned in Book One.

_____ 00695114 Book 1 – Book Only..............$6.99
_____ 00695113 Book 1 – Book/CD Pack $10.99
_____ 00695116 Book 2 – Book Only..............$6.95
_____ 00695115 Book 2 – Book/CD Pack $10.95
_____ 00699202 Book 3 – Book Only..............$7.95
_____ 00695117 Book 3 – Book/CD Pack $10.95
_____ 00695119 Composite Book/CD Pack.....$29.99

ANDRES SEGOVIA – 20 STUDIES FOR GUITAR

Sor/Segovia

20 studies for the classical guitar written by Beethoven's contemporary, Fernando Sor, revised, edited and fingered by the great classical guitarist Andres Segovia. These essential repertoire pieces continue to be used by teachers and students to build solid classical technique. Features a 50-minute demonstration CD.

_____ 00695012 Book/CD Pack.....................$18.95
_____ 00006363 Book Only $7.95

THE FRANCISCO TÁRREGA COLLECTION
INCLUDES TAB

edited and performed by Paul Henry

Considered the father of modern classical guitar, Francisco Tárrega revolutionized guitar technique and composed a wealth of music that will be a cornerstone of classical guitar repertoire for centuries to come. This unique book/ CD pack features 14 of his most outstanding pieces in standard notation and tab, edited and performed on CD by virtuoso Paul Henry. Includes: Adelita • Capricho Árabe • Estudio Brillante • Grand Jota • Lágrima • Malagueña • María • Recuerdos de la Alhambra • Tango • and more, plus bios of Tárrega and Henry.

_____ 00698993 Book/CD Pack.....................$19.99